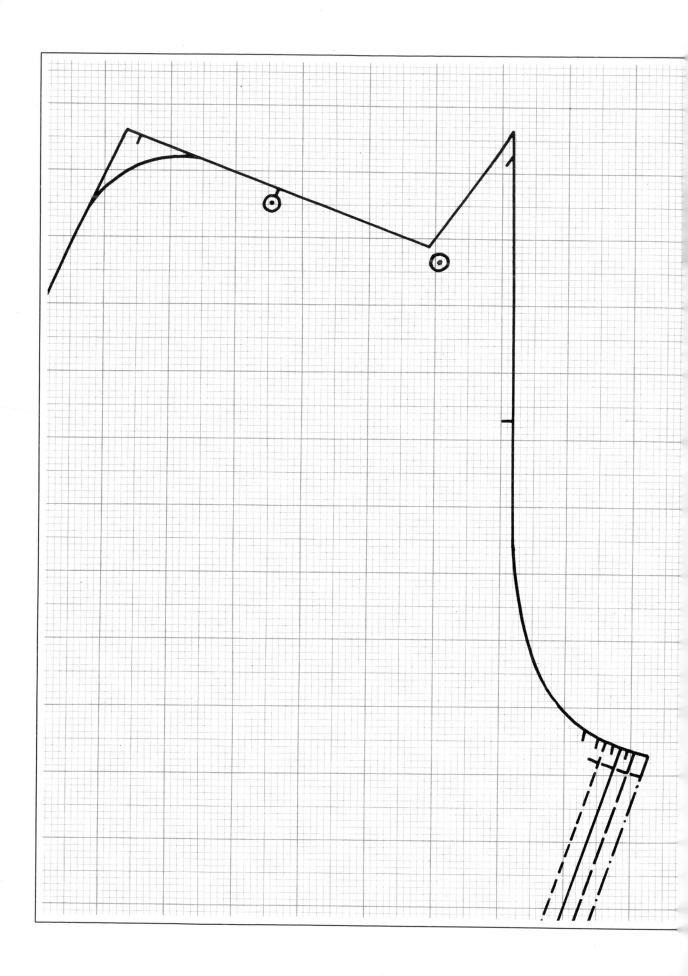

# CHARMIAN WATKINS

# DRESSMAKING BY DESIGN

## Stylish Patterns to Flatter Your Figure

EBURY PRESS
LONDON

**Published by Ebury Press**
Division of The National Magazine Company Ltd
Colquhoun House
27–37 Broadwick Street
London W1V 1FR

First impression 1988
Copyright © 1988 Charmian Watkins

ISBN  0 85223 619 0

**Senior Editor:** Fiona MacIntyre
**Editor:** Deborah Evans
**Art director:** Frank Phillips
**Designer:** Peter Laws

Filmset by Advanced Filmsetters (Glasgow) Ltd
Printed and bound in Italy by New Interlitho S.p.a., Milan

# CONTENTS

# INTRODUCTION

Although much has been done by designers in recent years to make it easier to co-ordinate separates successfully, very little has been offered to home dressmakers in the way of capsule collections.

Which jacket goes with which skirt? Can I get away with a full skirt if I have big hips? Will these two patterns go together? All these questions are difficult for home dressmakers to solve when they cannot stand in front of the mirror in the finished article. And making mistakes in your choice of design and fabric is often just as expensive as buying the wrong outfit. What is more, one cannot take it back and plead idiocy.

It is for all these reasons that I have put together a different concept in designer pattern books, one which will not only help you to plan and combine styles which will last for years, but against which you can check your personal body shape to make sure you are choosing the best for you.

In the book you will find a series of charts, listing figure points against which are set the best choice in designs; the three body shapes which appear time and time again are described in detail. One of these may well be you but there is also a chart which includes all the points, to help you if your figure is a combination of the three main types.

I have provided charts showing what design will go with what, both for day and evening, and there is even a chart listing basic accessories to help simplify the planning of your wardrobe.

You will notice from the designs within the book that each one comes in a basic 'Winter' form, with a 'Summer Version' based on the same shape with slight variations; for example, it may have a different neckline, collar or length. So the choice of designs, divided into twelve basic shapes, is actually huge and the whole collection has been very carefully worked out so that the different combinations possible are both highly fashionable and flattering. What is more, these designs are suitable for ages sixteen to sixty plus. From different combinations in the book you will be able to build a totally original and forward-thinking designer wardrobe, building on just a few capsule garments to create a collection of very original clothes.

I have tried, and I think succeeded, to go beyond the fashion dictates of the moment to create designs which will become classics and which can be recycled time and again in different fabrics and lengths. In short, the styles and information in this book will not become out of date.

Make use of the patterns, which are very easy to draw up to full size; none of the designs is difficult to make, and all can be attempted by a beginner. The Finishing details section allows you to choose your own favourite pocket and detailing shapes; I have simply given suggestions, but the decision is yours.

The Sewing techniques section offers all you need to know to sew these clothes professionally and there is a cut-out section in the back of the book to enable you to plan the designs you wish to make for each season. Pop these sheets into your diary or bag and take them with you when you go to choose fabric, buttons and accessories. They will make life easier and mistakes less likely.

I do hope you find the book useful. It should act as a constant companion to whatever style you wish to project in the future. Good luck and happy sewing!

# HOW TO USE THIS BOOK

CHARTS
TO
DESIGN

DESIGN
TO
PATTERN

PATTERN
TO
INSTRUCTION

## Making up the pattern
The easy-to-follow sewing techniques section on page 114 will help you with any queries you may have about the instructions for making up each garment.

## The figure charts
If you are not completely confident about what shape or style of garment suits you best, look at the figure charts on pages 8–15. This will help you pinpoint what your best features are and will identify which are the best patterns in the book for you to make up.

## The designs
The designs are shown on pages 18–66. Either flick through them as you would a designer's collection to pick out the designs you prefer, or use the figure charts to pinpoint those best suited to you. Each design has a winter and summer variation and can be made up in a range of fabrics with a variety of finishing details. Easy-to-follow making-up instructions are given on the pages following each illustration. They are accompanied by illustrations, where necessary, and give advice on the best fabrics and details for each design.

## The patterns
Drawn up on graph paper, the patterns for all the designs in the book are given on pages 78–107; this includes patterns for finishing details like pockets and belts. The patterns have to be scaled up to the correct size for you, and full instructions for doing this are given on page 114.

## Scaling up the patterns
Before you can scale up the pattern you have to make sure you choose the right size for your measurements. Use the chart on page 114 to find which basic size you are nearest to. Make a note of those measurements differing from the basic chart; the pattern pieces will have to be adapted once they have been scaled up to ensure a good fit.

# STYLING DETAILS

Once you have decided on the designs which flatter your figure, consult the following chart to see the various styling details that can be used to vary the basic pattern.

| | Shaped jacket (p. 18) | Straight skirt (p. 22) | Wrap blouse (p. 26) | Wrap skirt (p. 30) | Coat (p. 34) | Blazer (p. 38) | Casual top (p. 42) | Pants (p. 46) | Shaped dress (p. 50) | Full skirt (p. 54) | Shirt (p. 58) | Macintosh (p. 62) |
|---|---|---|---|---|---|---|---|---|---|---|---|---|
| Collar | ● | | ● | | ● | | | | | | ● | ● |
| Collarless | ● | | ● | | | ● | ● | | ● | | | |
| Choice of collar shapes | ● | | | | ● | | | | | | | ● |
| Round neck | | | | | | ● | | | ● | | | |
| 'V' neck | ● | | ● | | ● | | | | | | | |
| Boat neck | | | | | | | ● | | | | | |
| Single-breasted | | | | | | ● | | | ● | | ● | |
| Double-breasted | ● | | | | ● | | | | | | | ● |
| Sleeveless | | | | | | | | | | | ● | |
| Cap sleeve | | | ● | | | | | | ● | | | |
| Short sleeve | | | | | | | ● | | | | | |
| Three-quarter sleeve | | | ● | | | | | | ● | | | |
| Long sleeve | ● | | | | ● | ● | ● | | | | ● | ● |
| All-in-one sleeve | | | ● | | | ● | ● | | ● | | | |
| Set-in sleeve | ● | | | | | | | | | | ● | |
| Raglan sleeve | | | | | ● | | | | | | | ● |
| Wrap tie | | | ● | ● | | | | | | | | |
| Buttons | ● | | | ● | ● | ● | | | ● | ● | ● | ● |
| Zip | | ● | | | | | | ● | | | | |

| | Shaped jacket (p. 18) | Straight skirt (p. 22) | Wrap blouse (p. 26) | Wrap skirt (p. 30) | Coat (p. 34) | Blazer (p. 38) | Casual top (p. 42) | Pants (p. 46) | Shaped dress (p. 50) | Full skirt (p. 54) | Shirt (p. 58) | Macintosh (p. 62) |
|---|---|---|---|---|---|---|---|---|---|---|---|---|
| Wrapover style | | | | ● | ● | | | | | | | |
| Belt | | | | | ● | | | ● | | ● | | ● |
| Assymetric | | | | ● | | | | | | | | |
| Shaped | ● | | | | | | | ● | ● | ● | | |
| Straight cut | | ● | ● | ● | ● | ● | ● | ● | | | ● | |
| Flared | ● | | | | | | | | ● | ● | | ● |
| High waist | | ● | | | | | ● | ● | | ● | | |
| Waistband version | | ● | | | | | | ● | | | | |
| Elastic waist | | | | | | | | ● | | | | |
| Waist basque | | | | | | | | ● | | | | |
| Hip basque | | | | | | | | | | ● | | |
| Semi-circular skirt | | ● | | | | | | | | | | |
| Back interest | ● | | ● | | | ● | ● | | ● | ● | ● | ● |
| Top version | | | ● | | | | ● | | ● | | ● | |
| Choice of lengths | ● | ● | | | ● | | ● | ● | ● | ● | | ● |
| Seaming detail | ● | | | | | ● | ● | ● | ● | ● | | |
| Inset detail | | | | | | | ● | | | | | |
| Pleats | ● | | | ● | | | | ● | | | | |
| Inverted box pleats | | ● | | | | | | | ● | ● | ● | ● |
| Stitched pleats | | ● | | | | | | | ● | ● | ● | ● |
| Storm flap | | | | | | | | | | | | ● |
| Centre back vent | | ● | | ● | | | | | ● | ● | | ● |
| Finishing details | ● | ● | ● | ● | ● | ● | ● | ● | ● | ● | ● | ● |

Soft but slightly extended shoulder line detracts from big hips, creates balance

Rever and slanting pockets draw eye to body centre

Clever shaped seaming disguises a thick waist

Flared hemline minimizes big hips

# SHAPED JACKET

● This versatile, double-breasted jacket has extra front and back seams to flatter the figure. It is drawn in at the waist, flaring on to the hip, with a cut-away front hemline, all emphasizing the shape. Use fine wool fabrics for the winter version, adding extra interest with contrasting revers. The shorter summer version looks casual in linen, sporty in cotton poplin, or can be given up-to-the minute Chanel styling in delicate, hazy shades of bouclé.

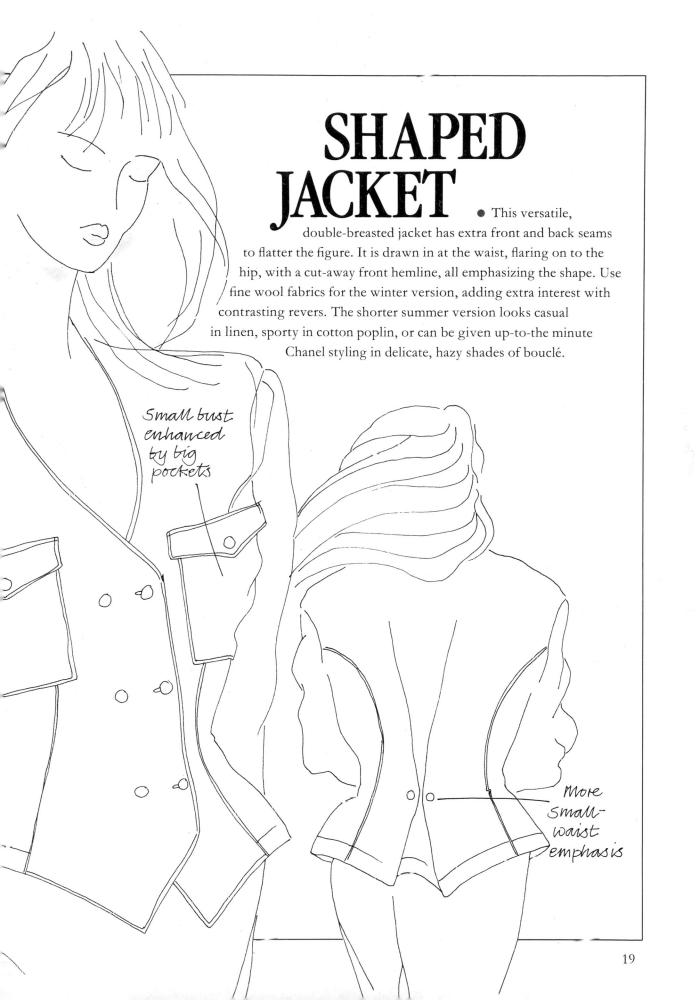

Small bust enhanced by big pockets

More small- waist emphasis

# SHAPED JACKET

**Fabric suggestions** Make up the jacket in ultra-fine wool worsted in intense dark colours such as wine, bottle, donkey or slate for the winter months – or choose a tweed and alpaca blend in natural greys and browns, adding toning velvet or satin finish wool revers for a chic finish.

For warmer days, choose delicate, hazy shades of bouclé for an up-to-the-minute Chanel look, or plain linen in natural mid-tones of olive, earth or sand for a more practical effect. Make it up in a sporting cotton poplin or gaberdine in apple, burnt orange or pillar box red with white highlights for a strong new summer look.

**Finishing details** suggested are an angled welt (no. 10) with an angled pocket bag (no. 12) for the winter basic version, and small patch pockets (no. 1) with a pointed pocket flap (no. 6) for the summer version (see pages 108–113)

**Pattern pieces** are on page 78.

## You will need:

|  | Winter basic | Summer version (s.v.) |
|---|---|---|
| 150 cm (59 in) | 275 cm (108 in) for sizes 10, 12 | 235 cm (92 in) for sizes 10, 12 |
| wide fabric | 295 cm (116 in) for sizes 14, 16 | 260 cm (102 in) for sizes 14, 16 |
| or 115 cm (45 in) | 335 cm (132 in) for sizes 10, 12 | 290 cm (114 in) for sizes 10, 12 |
| wide fabric | 345 cm (136 in) for sizes 14, 16 | 305 cm (120 in) for sizes 14, 16 |

(plus extra for optional Finishing details)

- shoulder pads
- 8 buttons (plus extra for optional Finishing details)
- 95 cm (38 in) interfacing for top collar and front facing (optional)

## Cut out fabric

**1** Draw up the pattern from the graph patterns on page 78, following the instructions on page 114. Cut out all the pattern pieces (see page 115).

## Back and front

**2** Join back jacket piece to each side back piece, right sides together, matching notches and easing around curves. Stitch from top to bottom. Neaten seam allowances separately and press open.

**3** Join each front to each side front jacket piece as in step 2.

**4** Make up and attach optional pockets and pocket flaps (see Finishing details, page 108).

**5** Join back jacket to each front jacket piece at shoulder lines, right sides together, matching notches and stitching from neck to armhole opening on each side. Neaten seam allowances separately and press open.

## Collar and facings

**6** For winter basic version only, make up collar as follows: attach optional interfacing to top collar, then set undercollar flat against top collar, right sides together, matching notches. Stitch from

point B around outer edge of collar to corresponding point B on other side. Clip curve of seam allowance (trim point if making a squared collar). Turn to right side and press undercollar and seam allowances away from top collar. Understitch along undercollar close to first stitching line, through seam allowances, from 2.5 cm (1 in) beyond point B (or beyond collar point if making a squared collar), along outer collar edge to same point on other side to set. Press flat. Baste top and undercollar together along remaining raw edges, matching notches. The top collar will roll over the undercollar slightly when folded into position.

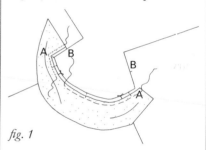

*fig. 1*

**7** For the winter basic version only, set undercollar against neckline of jacket, right sides together, matching notches. Stitch between points A. Clip seam allowance of jacket only to within a few threads of points A, then stitch from A to B on each side. See fig. 1.

**8** For both versions, neaten outer edge of back and front neck facings, down to lower edge. Join facings at shoulder lines, right sides together and matching notches. Stitch, neaten seam allowances separately and press open.

**9** Set facing against jacket at neck edge, right sides together and matching notches. Pin, then baste all round back neck to points A on each side. (On the winter basic version, the collar is sandwiched between jacket and facing.)

*fig. 2*

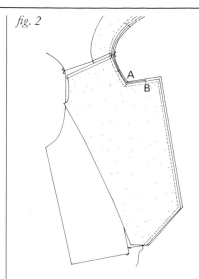

Continue basting through points B and around rever, down to hem on both sides (s.v.: from points A to hem). Baste across hem edges of front facings. See fig. 2. Stitch up and around neckline to finish as you began, clipping into facing allowance and pivoting the needle at points A for the winter basic version. Trim seam allowances, clip curves and trim points. Press facing and seam allowances away from jacket all round neck and front opening.

**10** On right side of facing, understitch through all seam allowances, starting 5 cm (2 in) up from hem edge on winter version (s.v.: from lower cut-away front points of jacket), up and around curved lapel edge (breaking stitching line 5 cm (2 in) each side of squared lapel) and continuing to just before point A. Begin understitching again beyond point A and continue around back neck

*fig. 3*

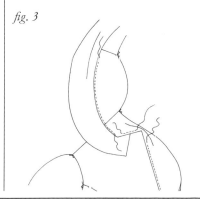

facing to lower front opening point. See fig. 3. (For summer version, begin as for winter basic and continue stitching up and around neck to finish as you began, breaking stitching line 5 cm (2 in) on either side of upper front opening points.) Press facing carefully to wrong side of jacket, setting shoulder lines together and joining jacket and facing armhole openings with basting, on each side. Pin, baste, then stitch inner curved seam allowance of facing to seam allowance of matching jacket piece to set in place, breaking stitching line for optional pockets beginning 5 cm (2 in) up from hem.

## Side seams and sleeves

**10** For winter basic and summer version, join back to front jacket at side seams, right sides together and matching notches, stitching from armhole opening to hem. Neaten seam allowances separately and press open.

*fig. 4*

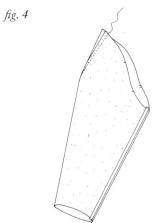

**11** Make up sleeves by joining right sides together at underarm seamlines, matching notches and easing slightly to fit. Stitch from underarm to cuff, neaten seam allowances separately and press open. Make darts in sleeve heads, folding right sides together, matching notches and dart markings. Stitch from armhole edge to dart point, tapering dart to nothing at point. See fig. 4. Neaten seam allowances separately and press open, pressing closed part of dart evenly to each side of seamline.

*fig. 5*

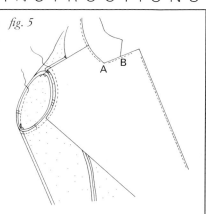

**12** Set each sleeve into appropriate armhole, right sides together, matching notches and underarm seamlines, and matching shoulder line to dart. Baste and stitch all round. See fig. 5. Neaten seam allowances together and press outwards, away from jacket.

**13** To finish cuff, neaten seam allowance at lower raw edge of cuff. Turn up along cuff foldline and baste into place. Edgestitch close to inner neatened facing edge of each cuff. Press.

## Hem, pleats and buttons

**14** To finish hem of jacket, neaten around lower raw edge of hem. Turn up along hem foldline, pinning then basting into place all round, tucking raw edge of hem facing flat behind inner front facing edge to neaten. Edgestitch close to inner neatened hem facing edge. Press carefully.

*fig. 6*

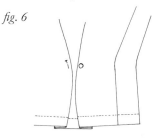

**15** Set centre back pleats into position, folding them towards the centre as shown in fig. 6. Attach a button firmly through each pleat.

**16** Make buttonholes and attach buttons as marked on your pattern and press completed jacket.

# STRAIGHT SKIRT

● A high-waisted, calf-length, figure-hugging straight skirt, designed to team with the shaped jacket for a winter or summer suit. The inverted pleats at the centre back and front allow for movement, and in the summer version, the circular hemline and shorter length give the skirt a more sporty feel. Either version may be made up with a waistband – a more flattering style for short-waisted figures.

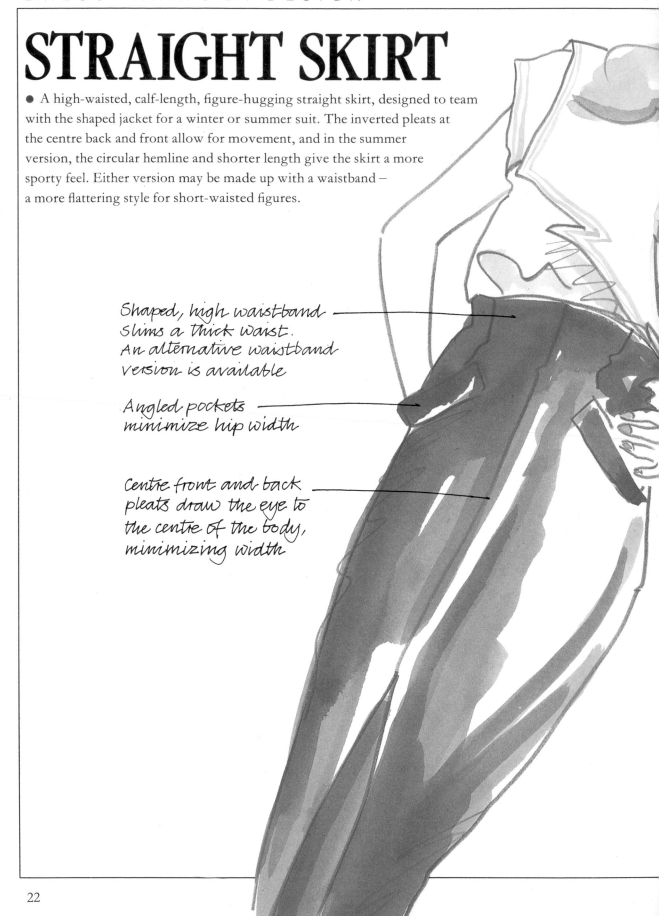

Shaped, high waistband
slims a thick waist.
An alternative waistband
version is available

Angled pockets
minimize hip width

Centre front and back
pleats draw the eye to
the centre of the body,
minimizing width

Flirty,
semi-circular
lower skirt
enhances
pretty legs

# STRAIGHT SKIRT

**Fabric suggestions** Use the same fabric as for the Shaped Jacket (page 18) to create a summer or winter suit, or use a toning linen to emphasize figure points (e.g. a navy skirt with a sand-coloured jacket to flatter weighty thighs). For everyday wear, repeat the design time and again in plain dark colours in wool or cotton gaberdine, barathea, worsted or flannel, or in cotton poplin for summer months. Totally transform the effect for summer by using tones of sand, burnt orange or donkey in cotton gaberdine, poplin or sailcloth. Natural, semi-abstract leafy prints would look equally good.

**Finishing details** suggested are small, straight pocket welts with squared pocket bags (nos. 8 and 11) or angled welts with small angled pocket bags (nos. 10 and 12) (see Finishing details, pages 108–113).
**Pattern pieces** are on page 80.

## You will need:

|  | Winter basic | Summer version (s.v.) |
|---|---|---|
| 150 cm (59 in) wide fabric | 120 cm (48 in) for sizes 10, 12, 14<br>210 cm (83 in) for size 16 | 145 cm (58 in) |
| or 115 cm (45 in) wide fabric | 210 cm (83 in) | 180 cm (71 in) |
| or 90 cm (36 in) wide fabric | 210 cm (83 in) | 195 cm (77 in) for sizes 10, 12<br>265 cm (105 in) for sizes 14, 16 |

(plus an extra 10 cm (4 in) for waistband version, and extra for Finishing details)

- 25 cm (10 in) zip (or 20 cm (8 in) zip for waistband version)
- waistband stiffening (optional)
- hook and bar
- 20 cm (8 in) tape for hanging loops

## Cut out fabric

**1** Draw up pattern pieces from page 80, following the instructions on page 114. Cut out all pieces in fabric.

## Back and front

**2** Make darts in front and back skirt pieces, folding right sides together and matching notches and dart markings. Stitch. Press all darts towards side seams.

**3** Attach front skirt pieces at centre front, right sides together, stitching from top to pleat opening point (s.v.: to bottom). Baste from pleat opening point to bottom notch mark. Press seam allowances open to pleat opening point.

**4** Make and attach optional pockets (see Finishing details, pages 108–113).

**5** Attach back skirt pieces at centre back, right sides together and stitch from bottom of zip point notch to pleat opening point (s.v.: to bottom). Baste from pleat opening point to bottom notch mark (winter basic) and from top to zip notch. See fig. 1. Press seam allowances open to pleat opening point.

*fig. 1*

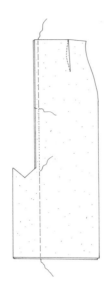

**6** Set in centre back zip by the hand-sewn, centred method (see Sewing techniques, page 120).

## Pleats

**7** For winter basic version only, set back skirt right side downwards on a flat surface and set back inverted

*fig. 2*

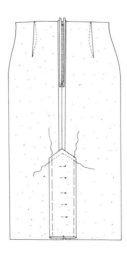

pleat in position, with centre back notch at bottom of skirt directly over the basting line. Pin, baste down each inner pleat fold and press into position. Neaten down each centre back seam allowance and across the diagonal top of each pleat. Stitch diagonally across the top of each pleat from pleat opening point to its outer edge, through to right side of fabric. Pull threads to inside and tie off to finish. See fig. 2.

## Circular hemline

*fig. 3*

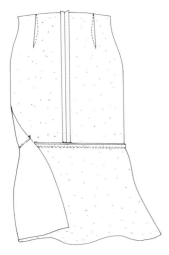

**8** For summer version only, neaten centre front and centre back seam allowances. Set top front of lower skirt piece against bottom edge of front main skirt piece, right sides together and matching centre front points. Stitch from side to side. Neaten seam allowances together and press upwards. On right side, edgestitch along main skirt piece and through seam allowances from side to side. See fig. 3. Repeat for back skirt.

## Side seams and waist

**9** Attach front to back skirt at side seams, right sides together, stitching from top to bottom. Neaten seam allowances separately and press open.

*fig. 4*

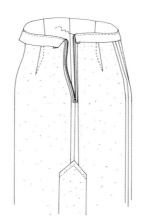

**10** To attach high waist facing, join the facing sections at centre front, right sides together, and stitch. Press seam allowances open, then set facing against high waist of skirt, right sides together and matching centre front points. Stitch all round from centre back to centre back. Press seam allowances upwards, then understitch along facing close to first line of stitching and through seam allowances, from centre back to centre back. Neaten inner raw edge of facing and turn to inside of skirt, folding under remaining raw edges at centre back opening to neaten top of zip. See fig. 4. On right side, edgestitch all round top of high waist. On wrong side, hand stitch facing flat to inside skirt at centre back zip, centre front, side seams and dart points. Press.

## Waistband

*fig. 5*

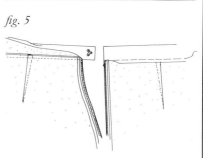

**11** For waistband version only, attach optional waistband stiffening to wrong side of waistband. Attach waistband to top of skirt, right sides together, matching raw edges and with centre back notches matching zip opening so that right back extension overlaps zip position. Stitch all round. Neaten inner raw edge of waistband. Fold short ends of waistband in half, right sides together and stitch across, pivoting needle at right back extension to continue stitching line to zip point. Trim corners and turn, setting flap over seam allowances with overlap of 1 cm ($\frac{3}{8}$ in). Baste into position, inserting hanging loops at side seams. On right side, edgestitch all round waistband and through to wrong side. Press and attach hook and bar at opening. See fig. 5.

## Hemline

**12** To finish hem, remove basting at back and front pleats. Neaten raw hemline edge all round (s.v.: turn under 5 mm ($\frac{1}{4}$ in) to wrong side and stitch all round). Turn hem to wrong side along foldline and baste all round. Herringbone stitch hem into position (see Sewing techniques, page 119) or machine stitch all round close to inner neatened edge and through to right side. Re-press pleats into position and press to finish.

# WRAP BLOUSE

● The sleeves and yoke are all-in-one, with above bust seaming detail. The wrap-over front opening which ties at the back of the waist make this blouse flattering to all but the very heavy-busted figure. The summer version is cap-sleeved and sports an oversized, softly cut collar.

Soft shoulder line and deep, all-in-one armholes minimize wide shoulders and thick upper arms

Large collar enhances a small bust and narrow shoulders

Waist tie emphasizes a small waist and creates a waist where there is little shape

Above-breast
seamline
disguises
a large bust

Pocket detail
enhances
a small bust

Three-quarter
sleeves shorten
long arms

# WRAP BLOUSE

**Fabric suggestions** This design must be made up in soft, drapable fabrics. Natural prints in mid-tones or warm, lazy pastels in lightweight, fluid lawns and transparent voiles would look fresh for spring, or silk satin or crêpe de Chine for evening, either printed or plain. Soft wool challis or crêpe in amber or deep petrol blue would highlight a dark suit.

**Finishing details** suggested are small, straight pocket flaps (no. 5) for winter basic (see page 109).
**Pattern pieces** are on page 82.

## You will need:

|  | Winter basic | Summer version (s.v.) |
|---|---|---|
| 115 cm (45 in) wide fabric | 310 cm (122 in) | 310 cm (122 in) |
| or 90 cm (36 in) wide fabric | 395 cm (156 in) | 380 cm (150 in) |

- two 50 cm (20 in) bias fabric strips, 5 cm (2 in) wide for cuffs on winter basic version
- buttons for optional Finishing details

## Cut out fabric

**1** Draw up pattern pieces from diagrams on page 82, following instructions on page 114. Cut out all pattern pieces in fabric.

## Sleeves, back and front

**2** Join sleeve pieces at centre back seamline, right sides together, stitching from top to bottom. Neaten seam allowances separately and press open.

**3** Attach joined sleeves to back blouse piece, right sides together, matching centre back and notches, and stitch from side to side. Neaten seam allowances together and press upwards. On right side, edgestitch along sleeve pieces and through seam allowances close to first stitching line, from side to side.

**4** Make up and attach optional pocket flaps or pockets (see Finishing details, page 109).

**5** Attach each front blouse piece to front sleeves, right sides together, matching notches and enclosing optional pocket flaps. Stitch from each side to front opening edge. Neaten seam allowances together and press upwards. Repeat edgestitching as for back blouse.

**6** For winter basic only, make shoulder dart in each sleeve piece, folding right sides together and matching notches and dart markings. Stitch from neck edge. See fig. 1. Press towards back. Neaten seam allowances together.

*fig. 1*

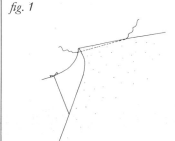

## Collar

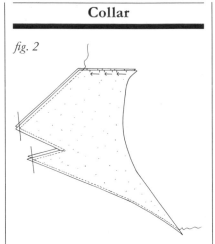

*fig. 2*

**7** For summer version only, make up collar as follows: attach left undercollar to left top collar along outer edge of collar, right sides together, and stitch. Trim points, clip seam allowance at inner corner as shown. See fig. 2. Turn and press carefully, allowing stitched edge of top collar to overlap undercollar slightly. Baste along shoulder line to set, then baste along neck opening edge and press again. Make pleats in collar shoulder line as shown on pattern, folding them outwards away from neckline, and baste. Repeat for right collar.

*fig. 3*

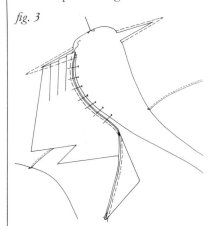

**8** For summer version only, carefully split shoulder line dart to split point as shown on pattern. Lay pleated collar shoulder line over shoulder line of blouse, undercollar to right side of blouse, so that its seamline lies directly over front seamline of shoulder dart. See fig. 3.

**9** Baste, then fold back of blouse over collar and front blouse so that right sides come together and collar is sandwiched between front and back bodice. Match shoulder dart seamlines, baste, then stitch across from neck edge notches to dart point and through collar seam allowance. See fig. 4. Neaten seam

*fig. 4*

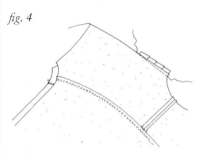

allowances together and press towards front, then on right side and with collar folded out of the way towards the back, edgestitch along front blouse shoulder line, edge of inserted collar and through seam allowances to set.

## Side and underarm seams

**10** For winter basic and summer version, join blouse at side seams and underarm seamlines, right sides together. Stitch from cuff to hem (s.v.: from armhole opening to hem), neaten seam allowances separately and press open, clipping at underarm points if necessary to ease.

## Edges and facings

**11** Turn under 5 mm ($\frac{1}{4}$ in) to wrong side at front opening edge of waist tie, stitching from marked point where lower edge of binding finishes, to tie point. Continue around hemline of blouse to finish opposite starting point. Turn under 1 cm ($\frac{3}{8}$ in) again and edgestitch all round, close to inner folded edge and through to right side. Press.

**12** Attach neck facings at centre back, right sides together and stitch. Press seam allowance open, then matching notches and with right sides together, attach to neck edge and complete as for bias strips (see Sewing techniques, page 117), stitching inner folded edge by hand to neaten. See fig. 5.

*fig. 5*

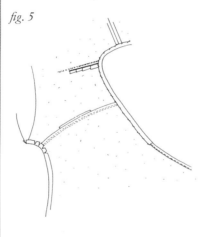

## Cuffs and armholes

**13** For winter basic version only, finish cuffs by attaching bias strips (see Sewing techniques, page 118). Press blouse to finish.

**14** For summer version only, join armhole facing at underarm point, right sides together and stitch. Press seam allowances open, then attach to armhole, right sides together and matching notches, stitching all round and finish as for bias binding (see Sewing techniques, page 118). Repeat for other armhole opening and press blouse to finish.

# WRAP SKIRT

● This pleated, front opening wrap skirt has the same softness as the wrap blouse (see page 26). Soft pleats at the front give the skirt a gentle shape, while darts on the hips give a flattering fit. The skirt dips at the front opening, for an asymmetric, mid-calf hemline. The summer version is transformed into a shaped and wrapped sarong with the addition of generous ties.

Simple, pleated wrap can be adjusted for any waist

Angled pockets minimize big hips

Asymmetric hemline gives added interest in centre of body

Darts at back of skirt give shape and fit, while tie disguises a tummy

# WRAP SKIRT

**Fabric suggestions** The winter version lends itself perfectly to a plain, dark-toned wool gaberdine or barathea for a tailored effect, but is totally transformed to give a casual, chic look by the use of a dark slate grey or donkey brown double jersey. For the summer version, a natural, leafy print or cotton batik design in blues, browns and soft greens creates a holiday mood.

**Finishing details** suggested are an angled welt with a small angled pocket bag (nos. 10 and 12) for the winter basic version, and medium patch pockets (no. 2) for the summer version (see pages 108–113). **Pattern pieces** are on page 84.

## You will need:

|  | Winter basic | Summer version (s.v.) |
|---|---|---|
| 150 cm (59 in) wide fabric | 200 cm (80 in) | 220 cm (88 in) |
| or 115 cm (45 in) wide fabric | 200 cm (80 in) | 220 cm (88 in) |
| or 90 cm (36 in) wide fabric | 285 cm (113 in) | 305 cm (121 in) |

(plus extra for Finishing details and fabric bias strips, if chosen)

- Bias binding or fabric bias strips for waistline facing, wrap opening (and for tie extensions on summer version)
- 2 hooks and bars for winter basic version
- 1 button for summer version

## Cut out fabric

**1** Draw up pattern pieces from the diagrams on page 84, following the instructions on page 114. Cut out all pattern pieces in fabric.

## Darts and back seam

**2** Make darts in each back skirt piece, folding right sides together and matching notches and dart markings. Stitch. Press all darts towards side seams. Set back skirt pieces right sides together at centre back and stitch from top to back vent opening. Neaten seam allowances separately and press open.

**3** Make darts on left and right front skirt pieces, stitch and press towards side seams.

## Front edges

**4** For winter basic version only, neaten inner edge of left front skirt piece. Turn neatened edge to wrong side along notched foldline, baste and press into position. Repeat for inner edge of right front skirt piece.

**5** For summer version only, turn back 5 mm ($\frac{1}{4}$ in) to wrong side at inner edge of left front skirt piece and stitch from top to bottom. Turn back 1 cm ($\frac{3}{8}$ in) again and stitch from top to bottom, close to inner folded edge. Press. For inner edge of right front skirt piece, attach long bias strip from top to bottom (see Sewing techniques, page 118) and press.

**6** Make and attach optional pockets (see Finishing details, pages 108–113).

## Side seams and waist

**7** Join back to front skirt pieces at side seams, right sides together. Stitch from top to bottom, neaten seam allowances separately and press open.

**8** For winter basic version only, set waist pleats as marked on pattern or to fit, folding them towards skirt opening. Hand stitch invisibly into place.

*fig. 1*

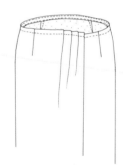

**9** For both winter basic and summer version, attach shorter bias strip to waistline of skirt (see Sewing techniques, page 118), turning in short ends to neaten. Fig. 1 shows winter version with pleats and bound waist.

## Ties

**10** For summer version only, attach two short bias strips to two long diagonal edges of left front skirt tie (see Sewing techniques). Fold remaining raw edge into 2.5 cm (1 in) deep pleats pressed upwards to make a total finished depth of about 10 cm (4 in). Neaten pleated raw edge and set right sides together against left front skirt as marked, with tie point facing towards side seam. Stitch through pleats from top to bottom. See fig. 2. Fold pleated tie back to right side and topstitch down pleats, 1 cm ($\frac{3}{8}$ in) in from previous line of stitching to set in place.

*fig. 2*

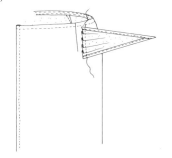

## Vent and hemline

**11** Neaten all round bottom of hemline and up each side of back vent opening (s.v.: turn in 5 mm ($\frac{1}{4}$ in) to wrong side and stitch all round). Place back skirt right side down on a flat surface. Fold right

*fig. 3*

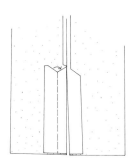

and left back vent openings to wrong side down seamline and press. See fig. 3.

**12** To set vent, pin, then baste left back vent opening into position. Fold right back vent facing to wrong side of right back vent along foldline. Position folded right back vent over left back vent. Pin and baste into position. Press flat carefully, clipping into seam allowance above vent to ease. Baste diagonally from seamline at vent opening to foldline of right vent facing. See fig. 4.

*fig. 4*

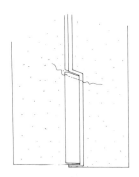

**13** Topstitch diagonally from seamline at opening point to foldline of vent facing and through to right side, to set in place. Remove basting. See fig. 5.

*fig. 5*

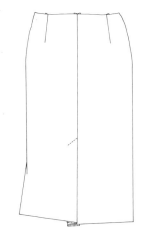

**14** Turn back the vent facings along foldlines so that the right sides come together. Stitch across each vent and facing along hemline. Trim facing seam allowance, turn and press. See fig. 6. Fold up hem along hemline and pin, then baste into position. Herringbone stitch (see Sewing techniques, page 119) all round hem and up each vent opening edge to set (s.v.: edgestitch along inner folded edge). Press.

*fig. 6*

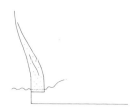

## Waist fastenings

**15** For winter basic only, set hook behind pleats at waistline of right front opening and stitch into place. Set bar to match on left front opening of skirt, over dart position or to fit. Attach hook (s.v.: button) to right side of left front skirt at waistline opening, adjusting to fit, and set bar (s.v.: buttonhole) to match on right side of right front waistline to finish.

# COAT

● This loosely cut, unlined coat drops to just above the ankle. It is double breasted and for winter warmth has a dramatic, oversized collar with cut-away 'V' detail at the centre of the back. The summer version is mid-calf length and sports an exaggerated roll collar with a curved finish at the centre back and a simple, unbuttoned wrap opening with belt. Choose fabrics in colours to tone with the rest of your wardrobe to give you a co-ordinated, layered look.

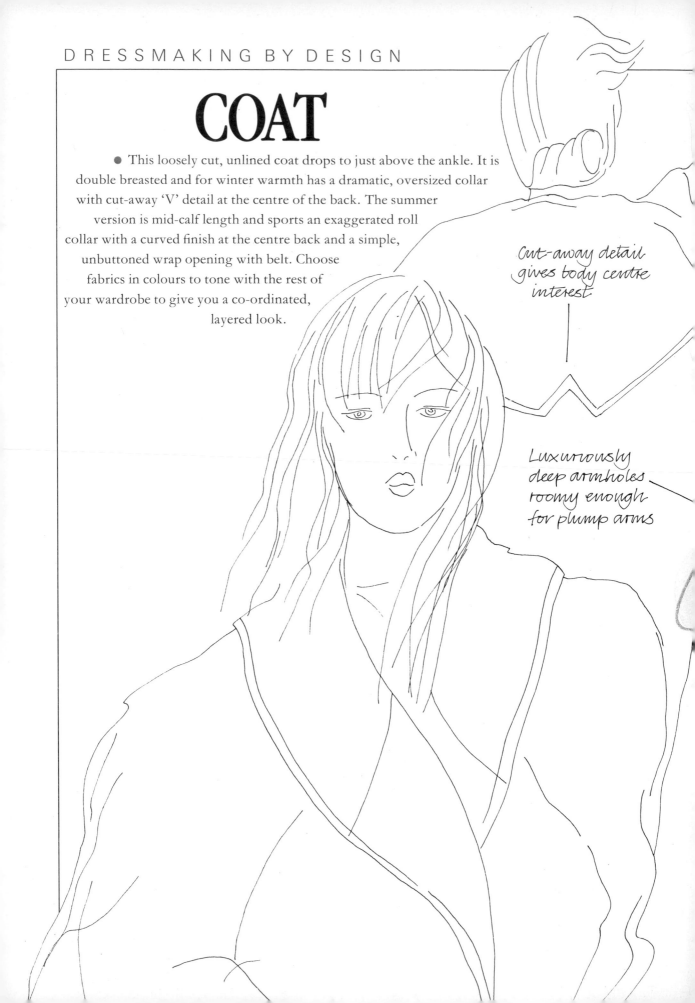

Cut-away detail gives body centre interest

Luxuriously deep armholes roomy enough for plump arms

Big collar
enhances
all shapes,
draws eye
away from
large hips
and bottom

Angled pockets
minimize
hip width,
as does
double-breasting

# BLAZER

● An easily structured blazer with deep, all-in-one sleeves, the basic winter version is 'V'-necked, with centre front buttons, while the summer version has a round neckline. Interesting angled and topstitched seamlines minimize hips and draw the eye towards the shoulders without over-emphasis.

Softly extended shoulder line detracts from big hips or bottom

'V' neckline elongates a short neck

Deep armholes minimimize plump upper arms

Front and back angled seamlines slim large hips and bottom, placing emphasis on upper body

vertical pockets
help to minimize
hip width

39

# BLAZER

Choose sophisticated double wool jersey in dark tones, with metal buttons for winter, or transform the style into a beach-casual look by the use of deckchair striped cotton canvas in vivid apple green and white, or red and cream stripes. Or combine toning colours to emphasize the angled side panels, adding a club badge or emblem for authenticity.

**Finishing details** suggested are medium patch pockets (no. 2) for the winter basic version and a single small patch pocket (no. 1) with a pair of vertical, welted pockets with squared pocket bags (nos. 9 and 11) for the summer version.
**Pattern pieces** are on page 86.

## You will need:

| | Winter basic | Summer version (s.v.) |
| --- | --- | --- |
| 150 cm (59 in) wide fabric | 255 cm (100 in) including pockets | 255 cm (100 in) including pockets |

- 4 buttons; 6 buttons for summer version (plus extra for Finishing details)
- 100 cm (40 in) interfacing for front and back neck opening plackets (optional)
- shoulder pads (optional)

## Cut out fabric

**1** Draw up pattern pieces from the diagrams on page 86 following the instructions on page 114. Cut out all pattern pieces in fabric.

## Front and back

*fig. 1*

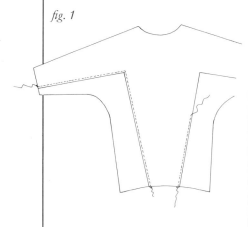

**2** Attach back blazer to each side back blazer piece, right sides together and matching notches, stitching from cuff to angle of seam. Pivot needle in fabric, clip seam allowance of back blazer only to within a few threads of point, and continue stitching line to hem. Neaten seam allowances together and press away from side back blazer piece. On right side, edgestitch along back blazer piece close to first line of stitching and through all seam allowances. Repeat for other side. Press. See fig. 1.

**3** Attach each front blazer piece to each side front piece exactly as for back. See step 2.

**4** Make up and attach optional pockets (see Finishing details, pages 108–109).

**5** Join back to front blazer sections at shoulder lines, right sides together, matching notches, stitching from neck edge to cuff down each side. Neaten seam allowances together and press towards back. On right side, edgestitch along back blazer close to first stitching line and through seam allowances from neck to cuff, on each side of blazer.

## Plackets

**6** Apply optional interfacing to top of neck opening plackets.

*fig. 2*

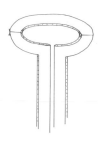

**7** Attach one back to one front neck opening placket at right shoulderline, right sides together and stitch across. Repeat for placket facing, then repeat for left side. See fig. 2 (s.v.). Press seams open.

*fig. 3*

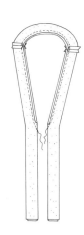

**8** Turn placket and attached facing so that right sides come together, matching notches. Baste, then stitch around neck edge. See fig. 3 (showing winter basic). Clip curves, trim seam allowance of shoulder seams and press facing and seam allowances away from placket.

*fig. 4*

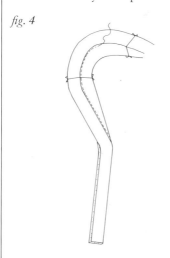

9 On right side of placket facing, understitch all round neck opening through seam allowances, close to first line of stitching, from 5 cm (2 in) inside front opening point to same point on opposite side. Press facing to wrong side. See fig. 4.

10 Attach placket to blazer neck edge, right sides together, matching notches, stitching from hemline up and around neck opening to finish at opposite hemline. See fig. 5. Press seam allowances towards placket.

*fig. 5*

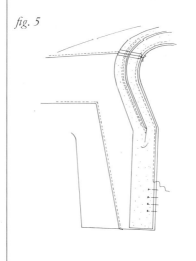

11 Neaten remaining inner raw edge of placket facing, turning in 5 mm ($\frac{1}{4}$ in) to wrong side and stitching all round, clipping to ease at corners.

## Side seams and cuffs

12 Join back to front blazer at side seams, right sides together and matching notches, stitching from cuff to hem. Neaten seam allowances separately and press open, clipping at underarm curves to ease flat.

13 Join one cuff facing at short underarm seamlines, right sides together, stitching across to form a circle. Set against cuff edge, right sides together, matching notches and underarm seamlines, and stitch all round. Clip curves of seam allowance, then press facing and seam allowances away from sleeve. Edgestitch all around facing from right side of facing, through seam allowances, close to first line of stitching. Neaten inner curved edge of cuff facing, turning in 5 mm ($\frac{1}{4}$ in) to wrong side and stitching all round. Press facing to inside cuff, baste flat to set, then edgestitch all round close to inner neatened edge of facing and through to right side to finish. Repeat for other cuff.

## Hem, buttons and shoulder pads

*fig. 6*

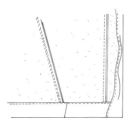

14 To finish hem, turn up 5 mm ($\frac{1}{4}$ in) to wrong side and stitch all round. Turn up hem again along hemline to form facing and baste into place. At front placket opening, fold bottom of placket and its facing right sides together and stitch across hemline, then fold back to right side so that facing folds to wrong side of blazer and encloses front raw edge of hem. See fig. 6. Repeat for other side. Baste along inner folded edge of placket directly over first line of stitching, to enclose all seam allowances, up and around neck edge to finish at opposite hem. Press, then on right side, topstitch up placket close to first line of stitching and through inner neatened edge of placket facing, all around neck edge and down to opposite hemline. Pull threads to wrong side and tie off invisibly, then edgestitch all around inner folded edge of hem and through to right side, aligning stitching with topstitching on plackets. Pull threads to inside and tie off.

15 Make buttonholes and attach buttons as marked on your pattern.

16 Attach shoulder pads with a few hand stitches and press to finish.

# CASUAL TOP

● For weekend and holiday wear, this top has a sporty feel, with its topstitched details and front 'V' inset for winter. All-in-one sleeves and angled underarm seams flatter the shoulders and bust. The summer version has short sleeves and is gathered into cuff and rib bands. Team it with blazer and pants for a complete outfit.

Cut-away
neckline
emphasizes
a slim neck

Angled
seamlines
slim large
hips and big
bottom, drawing
eye to centre
of body

Deep armholes
disguise plump
arms

Neck insert follows
angled seamlines,
emphasizing body
centre.

Cropped hem
emphasizes
a small waist

43

# CASUAL TOP

**Fabric suggestions** Match this top to the blazer (page 38) and pants (page 46), or make it up in velour, sweatshirting, cotton jersey or towelling for weekends. The winter version would look fresh in nautical blue and white striped cotton jersey, or could double as a serious sailing top if it were made up in blue cotton serge or lightweight canvas, teamed with the summer version of the pants.

**Finishing detail** suggested is a single small, rounded patch pocket (no. 1, page 108).
**Pattern pieces** are on page 88.

## You will need:

|  | Winter basic | Summer version (s.v.) |
|---|---|---|
| 150 cm (59 in) wide fabric | 180 cm (71 in) including pockets | 115 cm (46 in) |
| or 115 cm (45 in) wide fabric |  | 130 cm (51 in) |
| or 90 cm (36 in) wide fabric |  | 165 cm (65 in) |
|  |  | (plus extra for Finishing details) |

## Cut out fabric

**1** Draw up the pattern from the diagrams on page 88, following the instructions on page 114. Cut out all the pattern pieces in fabric.

## Bodice and sleeves

**2** Attach each side back piece to back piece from angle of seam to hem, right sides together, matching notches, stitching from top to bottom. Clip seam allowance of back piece into angle. Stitch remaining sleeve section of side back piece to sleeve section of back piece, matching notches. Neaten seam allowances together and press upwards and inwards, away from side back piece. On right side, edgestitch along back piece close to first line of stitching and through seam allowances, beginning at the hem, up around the angle of the seam to cuff. See fig. 1. Repeat for other side.

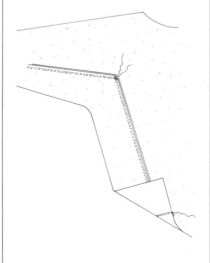

*fig. 1*

**3** Repeat step 2 for front and side front pieces.

**4** Make and attach optional pocket (see Finishing details, page 108).

**5** For winter basic only, attach centre front neck insert to centre of front piece, right sides together. Stitch from neck down one side to 'V' point at bottom, then pivot needle and stitch up the other side. Neaten seam allowances together and press upwards, trimming seam allowances of insert at 'V' point to flatten. On right side, edgestitch along insert close to first line of stitching and through seam allowances, from neck edge to point and up to opposite neck edge.

**6** For both winter basic and summer version, attach back to front pieces at shoulder lines, right sides together, matching notches, stitching from neck to cuff edges. Neaten seam allowances together and press towards back. On right side of right sleeve, edgestitch along back piece, close to first line of stitching and through seam allowances, from neck to cuff. Repeat for other sleeve.

**7** Join front to back pieces at side seams, right sides together and stitching from cuff to hem. Neaten seam allowances separately and press open, clipping into seam allowance at underarm to ease if necessary.

## Neckband and facing

**8** Attach one front to one back neckband at shoulder lines, right sides together and stitch across. Press seam allowances open. Repeat for remaining neckband, which will form facing. Attach neckband to edge of Top at neck opening, right sides together, matching notches and easing around curves. Stitch all round. See fig. 2. Trim seam allowances if necessary, clip around curves of seam allowance, then press seam allowances and neckband upwards.

*fig. 2*

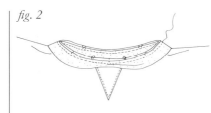

**9** Attach neckband facing to neckband at neck edge, right sides together, matching notches and shoulder lines, and stitch all round. See fig. 3.

*fig. 3*

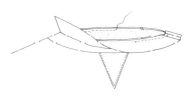

**10** Press seam allowances and facing upwards, then understitch along neckband facing close to first line of stitching and through seam allowances, all round neck opening. See fig. 4. Clip seam allowances on curves, trimming where necessary and press facing to inside.

*fig. 4*

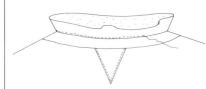

**11** Neaten inner raw edge of facing and set flat against inside of neckband, enclosing all seam allowances. Baste into position. On right side, topstitch around lower edge of neckband and through all thicknesses to set. Press. See fig. 5.

*fig. 5*

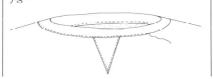

## Cuffs

**12** For winter basic only, join short ends of one sleeve facing at underarm seamline, right sides together, stitching across. Press seam allowances open. Attach to cuff edge, right sides together and matching notches and seamlines. Stitch all round. Press facing and seam allowances away from sleeve, then understitch around facing and through seam allowances, close to first line of stitching. Turn facing to inside and press. Neaten inner raw edge of facing all round, then baste flat against inside of sleeve and edgestitch all around sleeve, close to inner neatened edge and through to right side. Repeat for other cuff.

**13** For summer version only, run two lines of gathering stitches around sleeve opening. Join cuff at underarm seamline, right sides together. Stitch across and press seam allowance open. Attach one long edge of cuff to gathered sleeve edge, matching underarm seamlines, and stitch all round. Press seam allowances towards cuff, then neaten remaining raw edge of cuff and turn to inside along foldline to form facing. Baste into position, encasing seam allowances, then on right side, edgestitch around cuff and through seam allowances and cuff facing, close to gathered edge of sleeve. See fig. 6. Repeat for other side.

*fig. 6*

## Lower edge

**14** For winter basic, finish hem as follows: neaten lower raw edge of hem and turn up to wrong side along foldline. Baste into position, then edgestitch close to inner folded edge and through to right side all the way round. Press to finish.

**15** For summer version, finish lower edge of top by attaching rib band exactly as for cuff (step 13), gathering around rib line of Top. Press to finish.

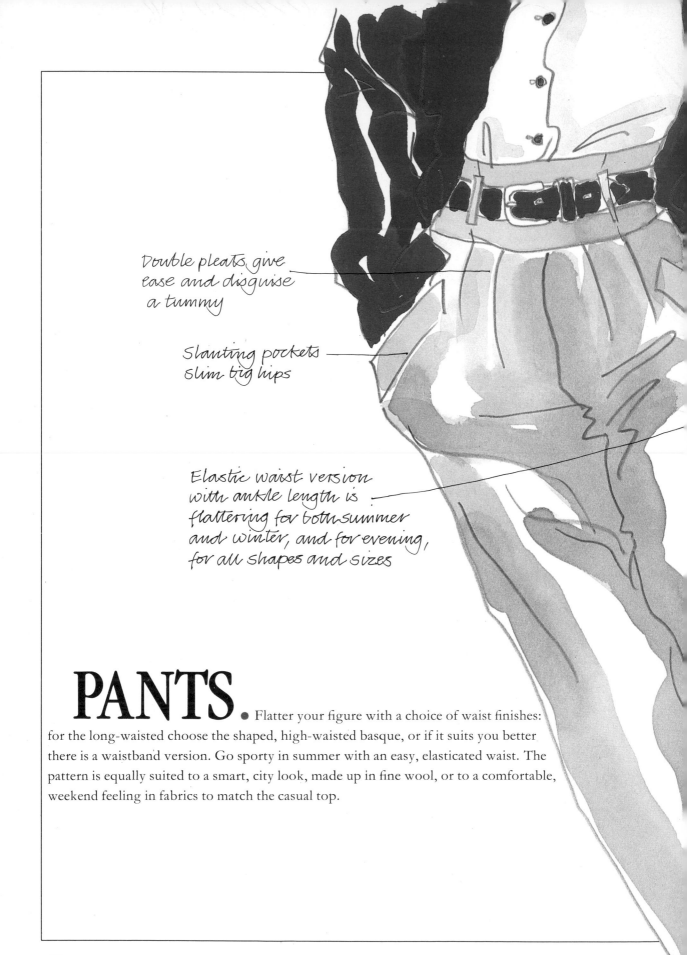

Double pleats give
ease and disguise
a tummy

Slanting pockets
slim big hips

Elastic waist version
with ankle length is
flattering for both summer
and winter, and for evening,
for all shapes and sizes

# PANTS.
Flatter your figure with a choice of waist finishes:
for the long-waisted choose the shaped, high-waisted basque, or if it suits you better
there is a waistband version. Go sporty in summer with an easy, elasticated waist. The
pattern is equally suited to a smart, city look, made up in fine wool, or to a comfortable,
weekend feeling in fabrics to match the casual top.

Minimum
fabric bulk
slims the
waist

Loosely
tailored
leg
minimizes
big thighs

# PANTS

**Fabric suggestions** Obvious fabrics to choose for the winter version include neutral and dark shades of wool worsted, barathea, gaberdine and flannel, while double wool jersey would lend itself perfectly to the elasticated summer version, as would silky jersey or crêpe de Chine for evening. Summer pants in small scale geometric patterns in dark greys and blues would make for smart city dressing, teamed with toning shaped jacket (see page 18) or shirt (see page 58).

**Finishing details** suggested are angled welts with small angled pocket bags (nos. 10 and 12) for the winter basic version, with belt tabs (no. 17) or large patch pockets (no. 3) for the summer version. (See pages 108–113.) **Pattern pieces** are on page 90.

## You will need:

| | Winter basic | Winter alternative | Summer version |
|---|---|---|---|
| 150 cm (59 in) wide fabric | 165 cm (65 in) for sizes 10, 12 | 125 cm (50 in) for sizes 10, 12 | 115 cm (45 in) for sizes 10, 12 |
| | 200 cm (79 in) for sizes 14, 16 | 160 cm (63 in) for sizes 14, 16 | 155 cm (61 in) for sizes 14, 16 |
| or 115 cm (45 in) wide fabric | 225 cm (89 in) | 230 cm (91 in) | 210 cm (83 in) |
| or 90 cm (36 in) wide fabric | 270 cm (107 in) | 230 cm (91 in) | 210 cm (83 in) |

(plus extra for Finishing details)

- interfacing for winter basic waist basque (optional)
- 25 cm (10 in) zip for winter basic (or 20 cm (8 in) zip for winter alternative)
- 2 cm ($\frac{3}{4}$ in) wide elastic for summer version
- waistband stiffening for winter alternative (optional)
- hook and bar for winter basic and winter alternative

## Cut out fabric

**1** Draw up pattern pieces from the diagrams on page 90, following the instructions on page 114. Cut out all pattern pieces in fabric.

## Darts, centre and side seams

**2** For winter basic and alternative waistband version only, make darts in both back pants pieces, folding right sides together and matching notches and dart markings. Stitch and press darts towards side seams. Fold pleats as notched in both front pants pieces, pressing towards side

*fig. 1*

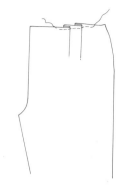

seams. Staystitch across seam allowance at top to set in place. See fig. 1.

**3** Join back pants pieces at centre back, right sides together, stitching from top to crutch. Stitch again just outside first stitching line to strengthen. Neaten seam allowances separately and press open.

**4** Join front pants pieces at centre front, right sides together, stitching from top to crutch. Neaten seam allowances separately and press open.

**5** Make and attach optional pockets (see Finishing details, pages 108–113).

**6** Join front to back pants at left side seam, right sides together, stitching from zip notch to bottom. Baste from zip notch to top (s.v.: stitch from top to bottom). Join remaining side seam from top to bottom, right sides together and stitch. Neaten seam allowances separately and press open. (S.v.: make and attach optional side-seam pockets (see Finishing details, page 109).)

## Basque and zip

**7** For winter basic only, make up waist basque as follows: attach optional interfacing to one front and one back piece. Make darts in two back and two front basque pieces. Press all darts towards side seams. Set interfaced front against interfaced back waist basque piece, right sides together and stitch down right side seam only from top to bottom. Baste left side seam in place and press both seam allowances open. Repeat to join remaining two basque pieces and set aside – these will form the basque facing.

**8** For winter basic version only, attach interfaced waist basque to top of pants, right sides together and matching centre front, centre back and side seams. Stitch from

_fig. 2_

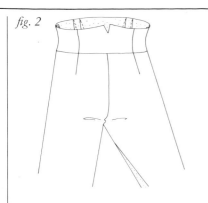

left front, right round to left back at basted zip opening and press seam allowances upwards. See fig. 2.

**9** For winter basic and alternative waistband version, attach zip to left side seam opening (see Sewing techniques, centred zip, page 120).

**10** For winter basic, set remaining basque facing against attached waist basque, right sides together, matching centre front, centre back and side seams and stitch all round. On facing, understitch around top and through seam allowances to set. Trim facing seam allowance only, then neaten raw edge of facing and turn to inside, clipping into seam allowance at centre back 'V' point to ease.

**11** Remove zip basting, then set facing in position flat against wrong side of basque, overlapping seam allowances to enclose them and turning facing inwards against zip opening to neaten. See fig. 3.

_fig. 3_

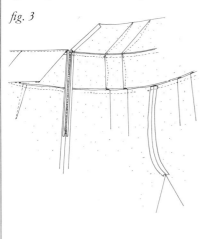

**12** On right side of waist basque at lower edge, edgestitch from left front zip opening to left back zip opening and through facing. Edgestitch again around top of waist basque. See fig. 4. Slipstitch (see Sewing techniques, page 119) down folded-in facing at zip opening to close. Press.

_fig. 4_

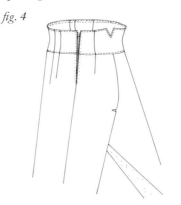

## Waistband or gathered waist

**13** For alternative waistband version only, follow instructions as for Straight skirt, step 11, page 25, omitting hanging loops.

**14** For summer version only, join waistband at short ends to make a circle, right sides together and stitch. Press seam allowances open. Attach one long edge to top of pants, right sides together and matching seamline to left side seam. Stitch all round. Press seam allowances upwards, neaten

_fig. 5_

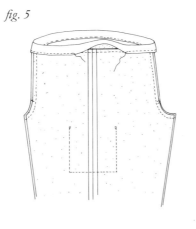

remaining long raw edge of waistband and fold over to inside, overlapping seam allowances by 1.5 cm ($\frac{5}{8}$ in) to enclose them. Baste, then on right side, edgestitch along waistband through to wrong side, close to first stitching line, leaving a gap at the left side seam through which to insert elastic (see fig. 5). Cut elastic to fit your waist, add allowance for stitching overlap, then thread through waistband. Stitch elastic at overlap to secure and finish edgestitching.

## Inside leg seams and hems

_fig. 6_

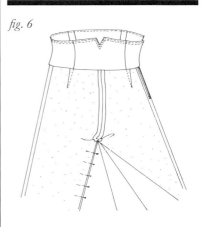

**15** To finish pants, turn to wrong side and attach front to back inside legs, right sides together. See fig. 6. Stitch from bottom of one leg, up and around crutch to finish at bottom of other leg. Neaten seam allowances separately. Press open.

**16** Finish hems by neatening raw edges, turning up to wrong side along hemline. Baste, then herringbone stitch all round (see Sewing techniques, page 119) or edgestitch close to inner neatened edge. Press.

# SHAPED DRESS

● Centre front buttons, a round neckline and inverted pleats at the hips make this a practical dress for everyday wear. Vertical seamlines enhance the shaping at the waist, while all-in one sleeves and horizontal seams at the bustline flatter the shoulders and neck. For summer, the dress can be made with cap sleeves, or cropped above the waistline for a simple top to team with the straight skirt.

Flattering, slightly cut-away neckline slims a thick neck, and draws the eye to the face

Above-the-bust seaming minimizes large breasts, while optional pocket flaps enhance a small bust

Softly curved
shoulders flatter
all shapes, while
three-quarter
sleeves shorten
long arms

Cut-away
version for
enhancing
slim waists
only

Curved
seamlines
emphasize
a waistline,
while inverted
pleats opening
from below the
hip minimize
large bottom
and hips

Centre front
opening
draws eye
away from
body width

# SHAPED DRESS

**Fabric suggestions** Brightly coloured cotton seersucker, stripes, gingham or a bright beach print would inject a '50s vitality into this versatile dress. A more sombre navy or petrol double wool jersey or crêpe totally changes the look for more formal occasions, emphasizing the shape and seaming of the design, with Art Nouveau buttons to complete the effect.

**Finishing details** suggested are small, straight pocket flaps, set into the seamline at the bust (no. 5, page 109).
**Pattern pieces** are on pages 95–97.

## You will need:

| | Winter basic | Summer version | Cropped top |
|---|---|---|---|
| 150 cm (59 in) | 335 cm (132 in) | 310 cm (122 in) | 110 cm (44 in) |
| wide fabric | (including pockets) | (including pockets) | |
| or 115 cm (45 in) | | | 130 cm (51 in) |
| wide fabric | | | (including pockets) |

● 8 buttons (4 for cropped top) plus extra for Finishing details

### Cut out fabric

*fig. 1*

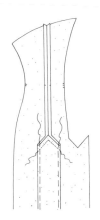

**1** Draw up pattern pieces from the diagrams on pages 95–97, following the instructions on page 114. Cut out all pattern pieces in fabric.

### Pleats

**2** Make darts and inverted pleats in each back skirt piece as follows: fold one skirt piece in half lengthways, right sides together, along dart foldline, matching notches and dart markings. Baste from top to pleat opening point. Stitch, neaten seam allowances separately and neaten around point of pleat top. Baste down inverted pleat foldlines from top of pleat to hem, matching pleat notches. On wrong side, press seam allowances open. On a flat surface, set inverted pleat panel evenly over stitching and basting line and pleat opening point, so that pleat edges overlap central line equally. Press. On right side, baste each fold of the pleat flat into position against skirt. On wrong side, stitch across top of

pleat in a 'V' shape to secure. See fig. 1. Repeat for other back skirt piece.

**3** Attach back skirt pieces at centre back seamline, right sides together and matching notches, stitching from top to pleat opening point. Continue stitching around top of centre back pleat, right sides together and stitch down to centre

*fig. 2*

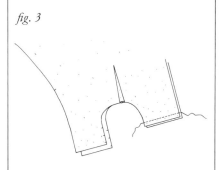

back split point. Baste from pleat opening point down inverted pleat foldlines as before, to hem. Continue as for previous inverted pleats, pressing and basting into position. Press centre back seamline of pleat, then press centre back split facings to wrong side along foldlines. See fig. 2.

**4** Make darts and inverted pleats in both front skirt pieces as for back skirt (step 2).

### Sleeves

*fig. 3*

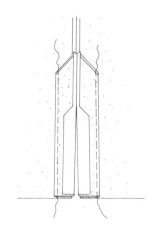

**5** Make shoulder darts in each sleeve piece, folding right sides together and matching notches and dart markings. Stitch from neck edge to outer dart point. Press darts evenly to each side of stitching line.

Join the two sleeve pieces at centre back, right sides together, stitching from top to bottom. Neaten seam allowances separately and press open. See fig. 3.

**6** Make and attach optional pocket flaps to front skirt pieces if required, placing them centrally over darts at top of skirt.

**7** Attach joined sleeve pieces to skirt at back, right sides together and matching centre back points, stitching from one side to the other. Neaten seam allowances together and press upwards. On right side, edgestitch from side to side of back sleeve pieces, through all seam allowances, close to first line of stitching.

**8** Attach front sleeve pieces to front skirt pieces, matching front foldline notches and dart notches, stitching from underarm to front opening edge on each side. Enclose seam allowance of pocket flaps if used. Neaten seam allowances together and press upwards.

**9** Neaten front opening facing edge from top to bottom of dress, then fold back along foldline, basting and pressing into position. On right side of each front sleeve piece, edgestitch from underarm to front opening fold on each side, close to first line of stitching and through all seam allowances and front opening facings. Pull threads to inside at front openings and tie off invisibly. See fig. 4.

*fig. 4*

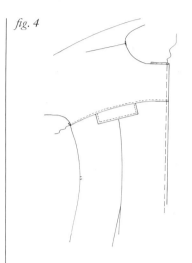

## Side seams and neckline

**10** Join back to each front at side seams, right sides together and matching notches, stitching from cuff (s.v.: from armhole opening) to hem. Neaten seam allowances separately and press open.

**11** Neaten outer curved edge of neck facing. Attach to neck edge, right sides together and matching notches. Baste, basting down short front edge of neck facing to attach to front opening facing, right sides together and matching notches. Stitch all round. With facing right side uppermost and seam allowances pressed towards facing, understitch around facing close to first line of stitching and through all seam allowances to set. Clip curved seam allowances, trim seam allowance at centre back, then turn facing to inside and press flat against wrong side of neckline. Hand stitch facing to centre back and shoulder darts to hold in place. (For summer version, optional edgestitching can be applied around neck edge. Pull threads to inside at front opening and tie off invisibly.)

**12** For winter basic and summer version, join cuff (s.v.: armhole opening) facing at short ends to form a circle, right sides together and stitch. Press seam allowances open, neaten outer edge of facing, then attach to cuff (s.v.: armhole opening), right sides together and matching notches. Stitch all round. Understitch around facing close to first line of stitching and through all seam allowances to set. Clip seam allowance on curves, trim seam allowances, then turn to wrong side and press into place. Edgestitch along inner neatened edge of facing, through to right side to finish. Press.

## Hem and front fastening

**13** To finish hem, remove basting from lower part of pleats and front opening, then neaten all round hem (s.v.: turn under 5 mm ($\frac{1}{4}$ in) to wrong side and stitch all round). At front opening, fold back facing along foldline so that right sides come together, and stitch across hemline. Trim seam allowance of facing and turn to wrong side. Repeat for other front opening, then repeat for centre back split opening. Turn hem up to wrong side along hemline, baste, then stitch all round close to inner neatened edge of hem, and through to right side, beginning at front opening and continuing up and around centre back split in a 'V' shape, to finish at same point on opposite front opening of dress. Press, then repress pleats into position. Remove all basting stitches and press again.

**14** Make buttonholes and attach buttons at marked points on pattern (see Sewing techniques, page 119) then press to finish.

# FULL SKIRT

● This skirt has a flattering high-waisted hip basque with cut-away detailing at the front-buttoned opening, flaring on to the hips.

 The line continues with inverted pleats, stitched to the hips, falling to mid-calf length for the winter version. The summer version shows how the length can be adapted to suit fashion trends, finishing here 51 cm (20 in) below the waist.

Short, flirty version
for good legs

High-waisted, shaped basque
emphasizes a slim waist
or creates the illusion of one,
while removing bulk for
maximum fit

Front-buttoning creates central
interest, disguising big hips

Below-the-hip inverted pleats
minimize the width of hips or
bottom. There is a centre back hem
split for maximum stride

# SHIRT

● A neat-collared shirt with dropped armhole and simple sleeves, both the winter basic and summer versions button down the centre of the front. A stitched, inverted pleat at the centre back adds ease and detail. The winter version has straight sleeves, while the summer version has cut-away, bound armholes. Clever use of finishing details and fabrics make this a versatile pattern.

Slim shoulders enhanced by slightly cut-away armhole

Loose cut suitable for big and small busts

Dropped shoulder line and deep armhole disguise plump arms, bony shoulders

Loose, comfortable styling suitable for wear with pants, shorts and suits

Small, neat
collar flatters
the face

# MACINTOSH

● Classic lines and a choice of traditional finishing details (epaulettes, belt, cuff straps and a storm flap at the back) make this an essential element of any wardrobe. Wrap yourself up for winter, or for a looser summer mac with squared revers, shorten the length and omit the styling details.

Epaulettes concentrate the eye upwards, enhancing bony or narrow shoulders, minimizing large hips

Deep armholes, inverted pleat and generous cut create more ease and luxury, minimizing body size

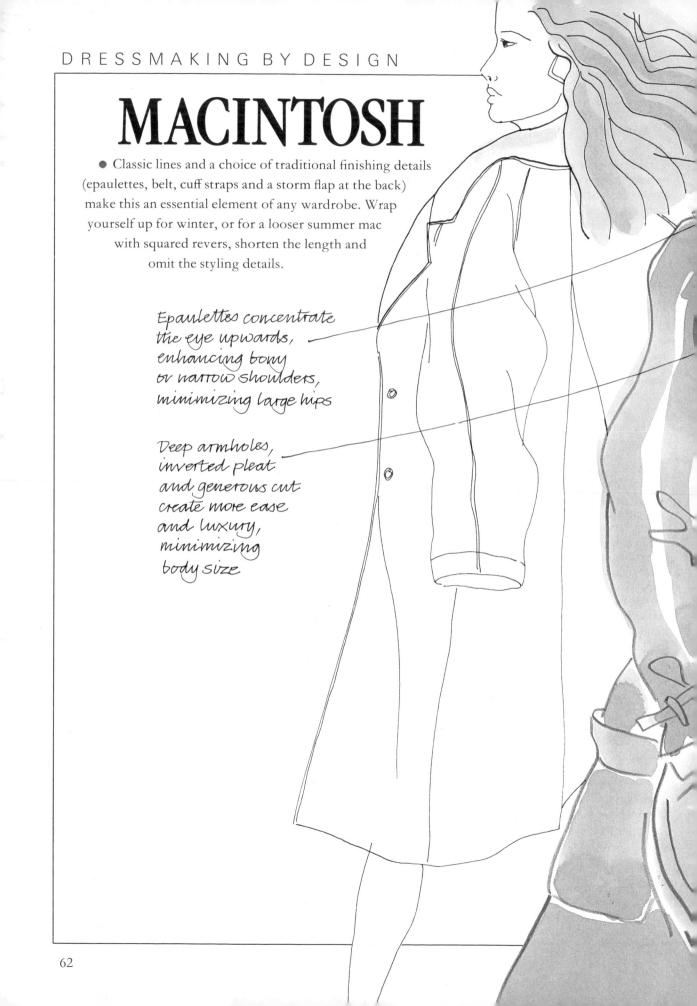

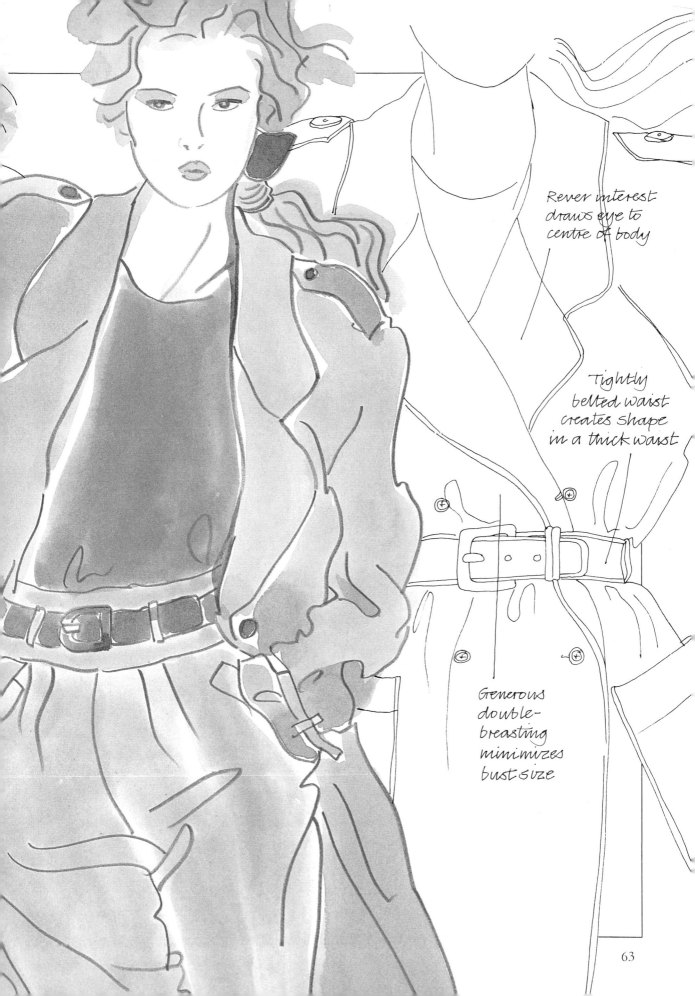

Rever interest
draws eye to
centre of body

Tightly
belted waist
creates shape
in a thick waist

Generous
double-
breasting
minimizes
bust size

# MACINTOSH

**Fabric suggestions** Neutral to dark shades in tiny checks or a plain weave are perfect for this design. Choose a proofed cotton, and add leather buttons and belt for the winter version. For summer, cotton gaberdine or poplin raincoating in light neutrals with horn buttons will give years of wear, or go for a stronger approach, in keeping with other garments in your summer wardrobe, choosing burnt orange cotton poplin faced with taupe or white.

**Finishing details** suggested are large, rounded patch pockets (no. 3) for the basic winter version, and large, squared patch pockets (no. 3) for the summer version, plus epaulettes (no. 14), cuff straps (no. 15), belt (no. 16) and belt tabs (no. 17) for the winter version. See pages 108–113.
**Pattern pieces** are on pages 102–105.

## You will need:

| | Winter basic | Summer version (s.v.) |
|---|---|---|
| 150 cm (59 in) wide fabric | 485 cm (191 in) | 410 cm (161 in) |
| or 115 cm (45 in) wide fabric | 695 cm (274 in) including pockets | 585 cm (230 in) including pockets |

(plus extra for Finishing details)

- 160 cm (63 in) interfacing for winter basic (135 cm (53 in) for summer version) for top collar, epaulettes, cuff straps and belt (optional)
- 4 buttons (plus extra for Finishing details)
- buckle (for winter basic)
- shoulder pads

## Cut out fabric

**1** Draw up the pattern from pages 102–105, following the instructions on page 114. Cut out all the pattern pieces.

## Details and sleeves

**2** Make and attach optional pockets (see Finishing details, pages 108–113).

**3** Attach interfacing to epaulettes, belt and cuff straps if required.

**4** Attach front and back sleeve pieces at shoulder line, right sides together and matching notches, stitching from neck to cuff edge. Neaten seam allowances together and press towards back. On right side, edgestitch along back sleeve, through seam allowances, close to first line of stitching from neck to cuff edge. Repeat for other sleeve.

**5** Join sleeves at underarm seamlines, right sides together, matching notches and stitch from underarm to cuff. Neaten seam allowances separately and press open.

## Back and front

**6** Join back pieces at centre back, right sides together and matching notches, stitching from neck to split opening point. Neaten seam allowances separately from top, down and around split opening to hem. Press open, pressing foldlines

into centre back split. Baste turnings into position down split opening.

*fig. 1*

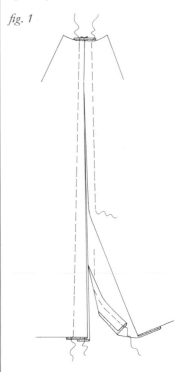

**7** Make inverted pleat at centre back as follows: fold down centre back seamline, right sides together and matching foldlines, so that the outer notches and pleat points come together. Stitch down foldlines from neck edge to pleat point. Baste from pleat point to hem. Lay back of mac right side uppermost on a flat surface and line up stitching and basting line with centre back seamline and split opening. Baste each side of pleat into position and press to set. See fig. 1.

**8** For winter basic version only, turn under 5 mm ($\frac{1}{4}$ in) at lower curved edge of back flap and stitch across. Turn under 1.5 cm ($\frac{5}{8}$ in) again to wrong side and edgestitch close to inner folded edge and through to right side, around lower curved edge of flap. Press and edgestitch on right side of lower edge of curve from side to side.

Position flap on back mac and baste around neck seam allowance and down each armhole, matching notches and raw edges. See fig. 2.

*fig. 2*

**9** Attach back to each front mac piece at side seams, right sides together, matching notches, stitching from underarm to hem on each side. Neaten seam allowances separately and press open.

*fig. 3*

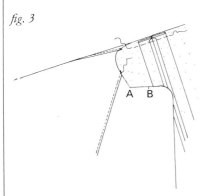

**10** Join left sleeve to left side of mac at armhole, right sides together, matching front and back notches and underarm seamlines, and enclosing seam allowances of back flap of winter basic. Stitch all round armhole from neck edge to neck edge. Neaten seam allowances together and press up, then on right side, edgestitch around sleeve armhole through seam allowances and close to first line of stitching, from front to back neck edge. See fig. 3. Repeat for other sleeve.

## Collar

**11** Attach top collar to undercollar along outer curved edges between points 'B', right sides together and matching notches. Stitch, then press undercollar and seam allowances away from top collar. On right side of undercollar, understitch close to first line of stitching and through seam allowances, between points 'B'. Clip seam allowance on curves (s.v.: trim seam allowance at points of collar), then turn collar to right side. Press. Baste from 'A' to 'B' on each side, matching raw edges and points 'A', then baste top to undercollar around neck edge between points 'A', matching notches and raw edges. See fig. 4.

*fig. 4*

**12** Attach collar to back mac at neckline between points 'A', right sides together, matching notches, with undercollar facing mac. Baste, then stitch into position. Clip mac seam allowances only at points 'A', then attach collar to rever on each side from points 'A' to 'B' and stitch. Press open seam allowances between points 'A' and 'B'.

## Facings

**13** Attach back neck facing to front facings at shoulder lines, right sides together, and stitch across. Press seam allowances open. Neaten facing along inner curved edges, turning under 5 mm ($\frac{1}{4}$ in) to wrong side and stitching from hem, up and around back facing to finish at opposite hem. Press.

**14** Set facing against mac around neck edge and front openings, right sides together, matching notches and shoulder lines and encasing seam allowance of collar. Stitch from hem, up and around rever and neck edge to finish at opposite hem, clipping facing seam allowance at points 'A' to ease. Press back neck facings and all seam allowances away from collar and mac.

**15** Understitch between points 'A', along facing and close to first line of stitching and through all seam allowances, to set back neck facing to inside mac. Press front facing seam allowances towards mac and away from rever, then continue to understitch along mac edge close to first line of stitching and through seam allowances, from just beyond point 'B' and around rever curve to finish 5 cm (2 in) above first button notch (s.v.: begin understitching below rever point). Press remaining front facing and seam allowances away from mac, then understitch

**Continued overleaf**

**Continued from previous page**

*fig. 5*

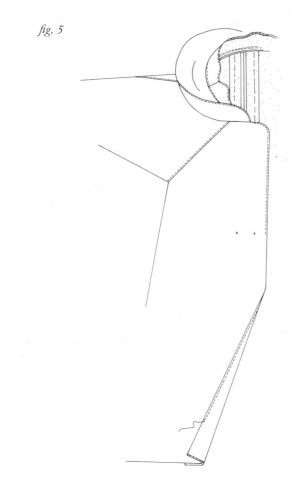

from 5 cm (2 in) below first button notch down facing and through seam allowances, to 7.5 cm (3 in) above hem. This understitching sets the rever roll and front closing into position. See fig. 5. Clip seam allowance on curves and press facing to inside of mac.

## Details and cuffs

**16** Make and attach epaulettes for winter basic version only (see Finishing details, page 112).

**17** Set and hand stitch a shoulder pad into position on each shoulder line.

**18** Baste facing into position inside mac, just inside neatened edge of facing, from hem all round to opposite hem. Herringbone stitch to set, starting and finishing 10 cm (4 in) above hemline on each side of front facing (see Sewing techniques, page 119).

**19** To finish cuffs, join ends of each cuff facing at underarm seamline, right sides together, and stitch across. Press seam allowances open, then neaten around inner curved edge of facing, turning under 5 mm ($\frac{1}{4}$ in) to wrong side and stitching all round. Press. Slip left facing round left cuff, right sides together, matching notches and underarm seamlines, and stitch all round.

Press facing and seam allowances away from cuff. On right side of facing, understitch all round close to first line of stitching, to set facing. Press to inside cuff. Baste all round inner neatened edge of cuff, then edgestitch close to inner neatened edge of facing and through to right side, all round. Repeat for other cuff and press to finish.

**20** Make and attach cuff strap to each finished cuff (see Finishing details, page 112).

## Hem and fastenings

**21** To finish hem, fold back front opening facing at hemline against front mac, right sides together and baste across hemline. Stitch, trim seam allowance of facing only to 2.5 cm (1 in), then turn back to inside mac. Repeat for other side, then repeat for each side of centre back opening split. Neaten raw hem edges by turning 5 mm ($\frac{1}{4}$ in) to wrong side and stitching all round. Press. Turn up hem along foldline to form facing and baste 1.5 cm ($\frac{5}{8}$ in) up from fold, all the way round. Press facing flat against wrong side of mac, then baste again below neatened facing edge and topstitch close to neatened hem facing and through to right side, all the way round hem. Press.

**22** Make buttonholes and attach buttons for winter basic version only as marked on pattern.

**23** Make up belt with attached buckle (see Finishing details, page 113) and make up and attach belt tabs as marked (see Finishing details, page 113) for winter basic only.

**24** Remove all basting stitches and press to finish.

# COMBINATIONS

By combining the garments shown on the previous pages in different ways, you can build up an individual wardrobe, tailored to suit your figure. Here and on the following pages, you will find some examples of the different outfits you can create, together with charts showing all the combinations available to you. The two sets of illustrations and charts show combinations suitable for evening and day wear. You will see how variations in the Finishing details help to create a totally different look for evening.

## Evening combinations

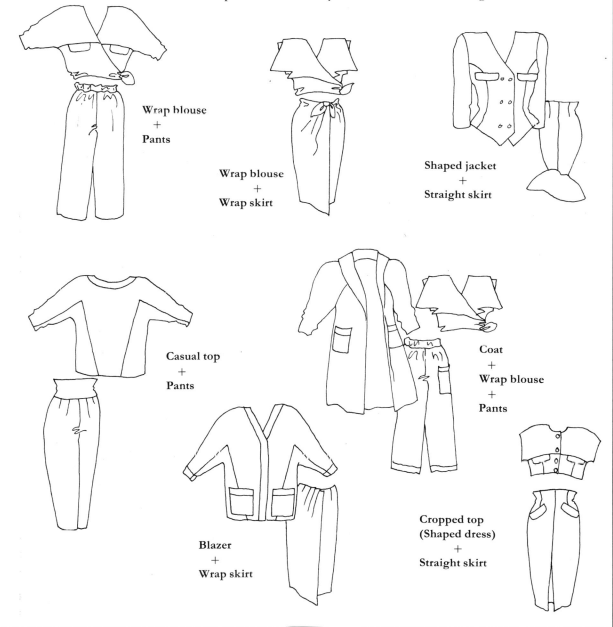

Wrap blouse
+
Pants

Wrap blouse
+
Wrap skirt

Shaped jacket
+
Straight skirt

Casual top
+
Pants

Coat
+
Wrap blouse
+
Pants

Blazer
+
Wrap skirt

Cropped top
(Shaped dress)
+
Straight skirt

● = suitable for combination

○ = illustrated combination

| | | Shaped jacket (p. 18) | | Straight skirt (p. 22) | | Wrap blouse (p. 26) | | Wrap skirt (p. 30) | | Coat (p. 34) | | Blazer (p. 38) | |
|---|---|---|---|---|---|---|---|---|---|---|---|---|---|
| | | W | S | W | S | W | S | W | S | W | S | W | S |
| Shaped jacket (p. 18) | W | | | ● | | | | ● | | | | | |
| | S | | | ● | ○ | ● | | | ● | | | | |
| Straight skirt (p. 22) | W | ● | ○ | | | ● | ● | | | | ● | ● | ● |
| | S | | ● | | | ● | ● | | | | | | |
| Wrap blouse (p. 26) | W | | ● | ● | ● | | | ● | ● | | ● | | |
| | S | | | ● | ● | | | ● | ○ | | ○ | | |
| Wrap skirt (p. 30) | W | | ● | | | ● | ● | | | | ● | ○ | ● |
| | S | | ● | | | ● | ○ | | | | ● | | ● |
| Coat (p. 34) | W | | | | | | | | | | | | |
| | S | | | ● | ● | ● | ○ | ● | ● | | | | |
| Blazer (p. 38) | W | | | ● | | ● | | ○ | | | | | |
| | S | | | ● | | | | ● | ● | | | | |
| Casual top (p. 42) | W | | | ● | | | | ● | | | | ● | ● |
| | S | | | | | | | | | | | | |
| Pants (p. 46) | W | ● | ● | | | ● | ● | | | | | ● | |
| | S | | ● | | | ○ | ○ | | | | ○ | ● | ● |
| Shaped dress (p. 50) | W | | | | | | | | | | | | |
| | S | | ● | ○ | | | | | | | | | |
| Full skirt (p. 54) | W | | ● | | | ● | ● | | | | | | |
| | S | | ● | | | | ● | | | | | | |
| Shirt (p. 58) | W | | | | | | | | | | | | |
| | S | | | | | | | | | | | | |
| Macintosh (p. 62) | W | | | | | | | | | | | | |
| | S | | | | | | | | | | | | |

| | Casual top (p. 42) | | Pants (p. 46) | | Shaped dress (p. 50) | | Full skirt (p. 54) | | Shirt (p. 58) | | Macintosh (p. 62) | | | |
|---|---|---|---|---|---|---|---|---|---|---|---|---|---|---|
| | W | S | W | S | W | S | W | S | W | S | W | S | | |
| | | | ● | | | | | | | | | | W | Shaped jacket (p. 18) |
| | | | | ● | | | | | | | | | S | |
| | ● | | | | | ○ | | | | ● | | | W | Straight skirt (p. 22) |
| | | | | | | ● | | | | ● | | | S | |
| | | | ● | ○ | | | ● | | | | | | W | Wrap blouse (p. 26) |
| | | | ● | ○ | | | | ● | | | | | S | |
| | ● | | | | | | | | | | | | W | Wrap skirt (p. 30) |
| | | | | | | | | | | ● | | | S | |
| | | | | | | | | | | | | | W | Coat (p. 34) |
| | | | | ○ | | | | | | | | | S | |
| | ● | | ● | ● | | | | | | | | | W | Blazer (p. 38) |
| | ● | | | ● | | | | | | | | | S | |
| | | | ○ | ● | | | | | | | | | W | Casual top (p. 42) |
| | | | | | | | | | | | | | S | |
| | ○ | | | | | | | | ● | ● | | | W | Pants (p. 46) |
| | ● | | | | | | | | | ● | | | S | |
| | | | | | | | | | | | | | W | Shaped dress (p. 50) |
| | | | | | | | | | | | | | S | |
| | | | | | | | | | | ● | | | W | Full skirt (p. 54) |
| | | | | | | | | | | ● | | | S | |
| | | | ● | ● | | | | | | | | | W | Shirt (p. 58) |
| | | | | ● | | | | | | | | | S | |
| | | | | | | | | | | | | | W | Macintosh (p. 62) |
| | | | | | | | | | | | | | S | |

# Daytime combinations

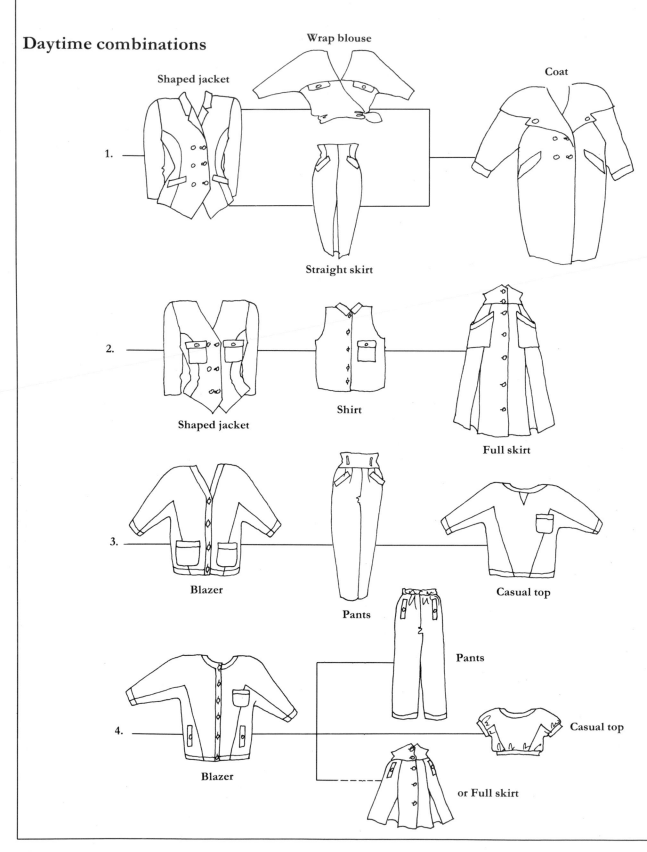

Wrap blouse

Shaped jacket

Coat

1.

Straight skirt

2.

Shaped jacket

Shirt

Full skirt

3.

Blazer

Pants

Casual top

4.

Blazer

Pants

Casual top

or Full skirt

5.  Shirt

    Pants

    Coat

6.  Macintosh

    Straight skirt

    Cropped top

7.  Wrap blouse

    Wrap skirt

8.  Wrap skirt

    Macintosh

9.  Shaped dress

    Shaped jacket

● = suitable for combination
○ = illustrated combination

| | | Shaped jacket (p. 18) | | Straight skirt (p. 22) | | Wrap blouse (p. 26) | | Wrap skirt (p. 30) | | Coat (p. 34) | | Blazer (p. 38) | |
|---|---|---|---|---|---|---|---|---|---|---|---|---|---|
| | | W | S | W | S | W | S | W | S | W | S | W | S |
| Shaped jacket (p. 18) | W | | | ○ | ● | ○ | | ● | ● | ○ | | | |
| | S | | | ● | ● | | ● | ● | ● | | | | |
| Straight skirt (p. 22) | W | ○ | ● | | | ○ | ● | | | ○ | ● | ● | ● |
| | S | | ● | | | | ● | | | | | | |
| Wrap blouse (p. 26) | W | ○ | | ○ | | | | ● | ● | ○ | | ● | |
| | S | | | ● | ● | | | ● | ○ | | ● | | |
| Wrap skirt (p. 30) | W | ● | ● | | | ● | ● | | | ● | ● | ● | ● |
| | S | ● | ● | | | ● | ○ | | | | ● | | ● |
| Coat (p. 34) | W | ○ | ● | ○ | | ○ | | ● | | | | ● | |
| | S | | ● | ● | | ● | ● | ● | ● | | | ● | ● |
| Blazer (p. 38) | W | | | ● | | ● | | ● | | | | | |
| | S | | | ● | | ● | | ● | ● | | | | |
| Casual top (p. 42) | W | | | ● | | ● | | ● | | | | ○ | |
| | S | | | | ● | | | | ● | | | | ○ |
| Pants (p. 46) | W | ● | ● | | | ● | ● | | | ● | ○ | ○ | ● |
| | S | ● | ● | | | ● | ● | | | ● | ● | ● | ○ |
| Shaped dress/ Cropped top (p. 50) | W | ● | ○ | | | | | | | ● | | | |
| | S | | ● | | ○ | | | | | | ● | | |
| Full skirt (p. 54) | W | ● | ○ | | | ● | ● | | | | | | |
| | S | | ● | | | | ● | | | | | | ○ |
| Shirt (p. 58) | W | ● | ● | ● | | | | ● | | | ○ | | |
| | S | | ○ | ● | ● | | | | ● | | | | |
| Macintosh (p. 62) | W | ● | | ● | | ● | | ○ | | | | | |
| | S | | ● | | ○ | | ● | ● | ● | | | | |

| Item | W/S | Casual top (p. 42) W | Casual top S | Pants (p. 46) W | Pants S | Shaped dress (p. 50) W | Shaped dress S | Full skirt (p. 54) W | Full skirt S | Shirt (p. 58) W | Shirt S | Macintosh (p. 62) W | Macintosh S |
|---|---|---|---|---|---|---|---|---|---|---|---|---|---|
| Shaped jacket (p. 18) | W | | | ● | | ● | | ● | | ● | | | |
| Shaped jacket (p. 18) | S | | | ● | ● | ○ | ● | ○ | ● | | ○ | | |
| Straight skirt (p. 22) | W | ● | ● | | | | | | | ● | ● | ● | ● |
| Straight skirt (p. 22) | S | ● | ● | | | | | | | | ● | | ○ |
| Wrap blouse (p. 26) | W | | | ● | ● | | | ● | | | | ● | |
| Wrap blouse (p. 26) | S | | | ● | ● | | | ● | ● | | | | |
| Wrap skirt (p. 30) | W | ● | | | | | | | | ● | ● | ○ | ● |
| Wrap skirt (p. 30) | S | | ● | | | | | | | | ● | | ● |
| Coat (p. 34) | W | ● | | ● | ● | ● | | ● | | ● | | | |
| Coat (p. 34) | S | ● | ● | ○ | ● | ● | ● | ● | | ○ | ● | | |
| Blazer (p. 38) | W | ○ | | ○ | | | | | | ● | | | |
| Blazer (p. 38) | S | | ○ | ● | ○ | | | | ○ | ● | | | |
| Casual top (p. 42) | W | | | ● | | | | ● | | | | | |
| Casual top (p. 42) | S | | | ○ | ○ | | | | ● | | | | |
| Pants (p. 46) | W | ○ | | | | ● | | | | ○ | ● | ● | ● |
| Pants (p. 46) | S | ● | ○ | | | | | | | | ● | | ● |
| Shaped dress/ Cropped top (p. 50) | W | | | | | | | | | | | ● | |
| Shaped dress/ Cropped top (p. 50) | S | | | ● | | | | | ● | | | | ● |
| Full skirt (p. 54) | W | ● | | | | | | | | ● | ○ | ● | |
| Full skirt (p. 54) | S | | ● | | | | ● | | | | ● | | ● |
| Shirt (p. 58) | W | | | ○ | | | | ● | | | | ● | |
| Shirt (p. 58) | S | | | ● | ● | | | ○ | ● | | | | ● |
| Macintosh (p. 62) | W | | | ● | ● | ● | | ● | | ● | | | |
| Macintosh (p. 62) | S | | | | ● | | | ● | ● | | ● | | |

73

# ACCESSORIES

| | | Sun cap | Saucer hat | Soft felt hat | Wrap sandal | Flattie | Court shoe |
|---|---|:---:|:---:|:---:|:---:|:---:|:---:|
| Shaped jacket (p. 18) | W | | | ● | | ● | ● |
| | S | ● | ● | | ● | ● | ● |
| Straight skirt (p. 22) | W | | | ● | | ● | ● |
| | S | ● | ● | | ● | ● | ● |
| Wrap blouse (p. 26) | W | | | ● | | ● | ● |
| | S | ● | ● | | | | |
| Wrap skirt (p. 30) | W | | | | | ● | ● |
| | S | ● | ● | | ● | ● | ● |
| Coat (p. 34) | W | | | ● | | ● | ● |
| | S | | | | ● | | |
| Blazer (p. 38) | W | | | | | ● | ● |
| | S | ● | | | | ● | ● |
| Casual top (p. 42) | W | | | | | ● | ● |
| | S | ● | | | ● | ● | ● |
| Pants (p. 46) | W | | | ● | | ● | |
| | S | ● | ● | | ● | ● | |
| Shaped dress (p. 50) | W | | | ● | | ● | ● |
| | S | ● | ● | | ● | ● | |
| Full skirt (p. 54) | W | | | ● | | ● | ● |
| | S | ● | ● | | ● | ● | |
| Shirt (p. 58) | W | | | | | ● | ● |
| | S | ● | ● | | ● | ● | |
| Macintosh (p. 62) | W | | | | | ● | ● |
| | S | | | ● | | ● | ● |

| | Walking shoe | Socks | Wool stockings | Pleated beach bag | Bucket bag | Large clutch bag | Oversize carryall | Leather gloves | Wool gloves | Wool scarf | Elasticated belt | Leather classic belt | Large brooch | Large earrings | Large bracelet | Watch | Big necklace | Sunglasses |
|---|---|---|---|---|---|---|---|---|---|---|---|---|---|---|---|---|---|---|
| | | ● | ● | | ● | ● | | ● | ● | | | | ● | ● | ● | ● | | ● |
| | ● | ● | | | ● | ● | ● | | | | | | ● | ● | ● | ● | | ● |
| | ● | ● | ● | | | | | | | | ● | ● | | | | | | |
| | ● | ● | | ● | ● | ● | | | | | ● | | | | | | | |
| | ● | | ● | | ● | ● | ● | | | | | | ● | ● | ● | ● | ● | ● |
| | | | | ● | | ● | | | | | | | ● | ● | ● | ● | | ● |
| | ● | | ● | | | ● | ● | | | | | | | | | | | |
| | | | | ● | ● | | ● | | | | | | | | | | | |
| | ● | ● | ● | | ● | ● | | ● | ● | ● | | | ● | ● | ● | ● | | ● |
| | ● | ● | | | ● | | | | | | | ● | ● | ● | ● | ● | ● | ● |
| | ● | ● | ● | ● | ● | | ● | | | | | | ● | ● | ● | ● | | ● |
| | ● | ● | | | ● | | ● | | | | | | ● | ● | ● | ● | | ● |
| | ● | ● | ● | | ● | | ● | | ● | | | | ● | ● | ● | ● | ● | ● |
| | | | | ● | ● | | ● | | | | | | ● | ● | ● | ● | ● | ● |
| | ● | ● | | | ● | ● | ● | | | | ● | ● | | | | | | |
| | ● | ● | | ● | ● | ● | ● | | | | ● | | | | | | | |
| | ● | ● | ● | | | ● | | ● | ● | | ● | | ● | ● | ● | ● | ● | ● |
| | | | | ● | ● | ● | ● | | | | ● | | ● | ● | ● | ● | ● | ● |
| | ● | ● | ● | ● | ● | ● | ● | | ● | | ● | ● | | | | | | |
| | | | | ● | ● | ● | | | | | ● | ● | | | | | | |
| | ● | | ● | | | | | | | | ● | ● | ● | ● | ● | ● | ● | ● |
| | | | | ● | ● | | ● | | | | ● | | ● | ● | ● | ● | ● | ● |
| | ● | ● | ● | | ● | ● | ● | ● | ● | ● | | ● | ● | ● | ● | ● | | ● |
| | ● | ● | | | ● | ● | ● | | | | | | ● | ● | ● | ● | | ● |

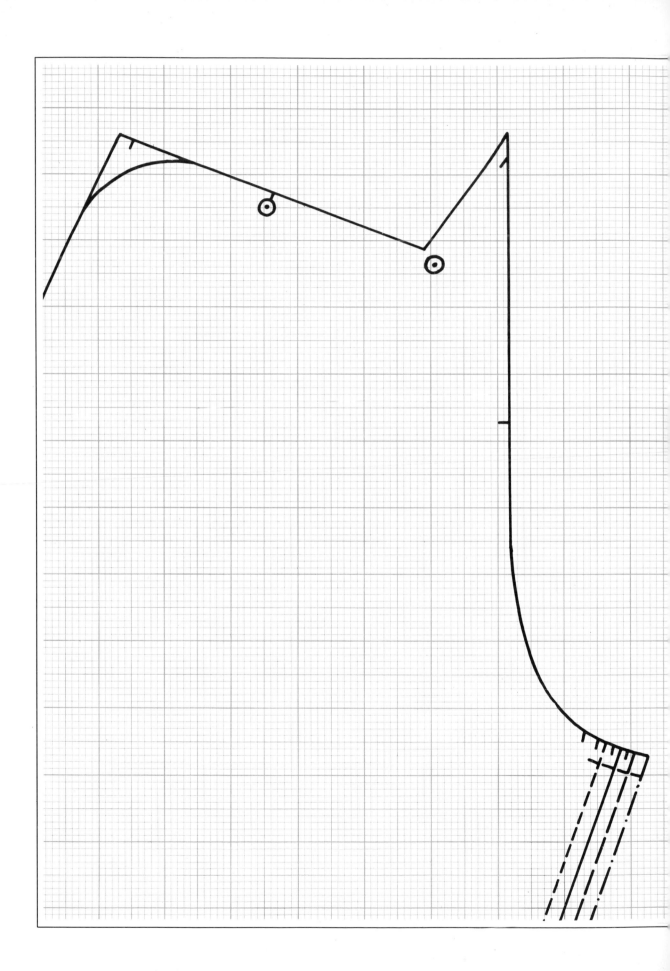

# THE
# PATTERNS

# SHAPED JACKET

*Illustrated on page 18*

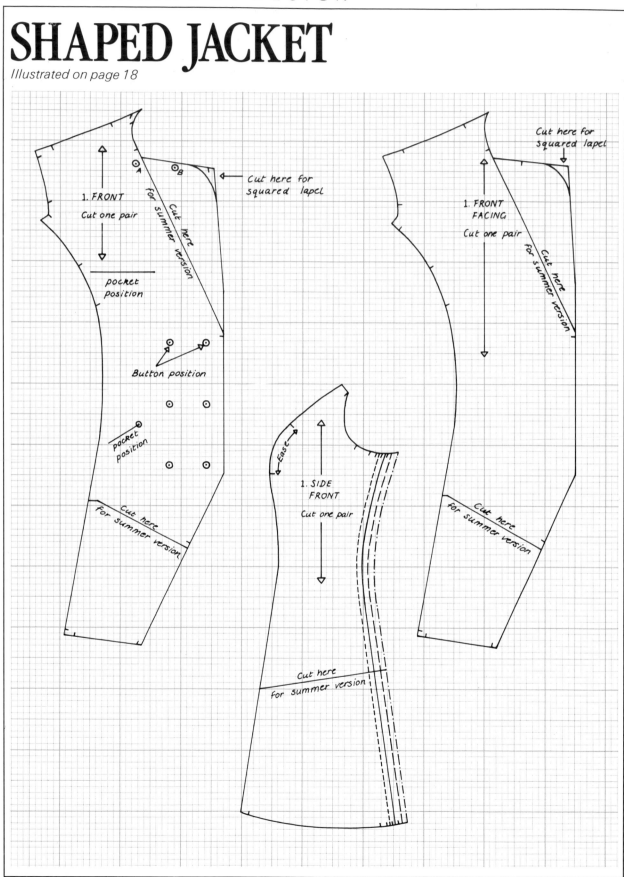

Cut here for
squared lapel

A
B

1. FRONT
Cut one pair

Cut here
for summer version

pocket
position

Button position

pocket
position

Cut here
for summer version

Cut here for
squared lapel

1. FRONT
FACING

Cut one pair

Cut here
for summer version

Cut here
for summer version

Ease

1. SIDE
FRONT

Cut one pair

Cut here
for summer version

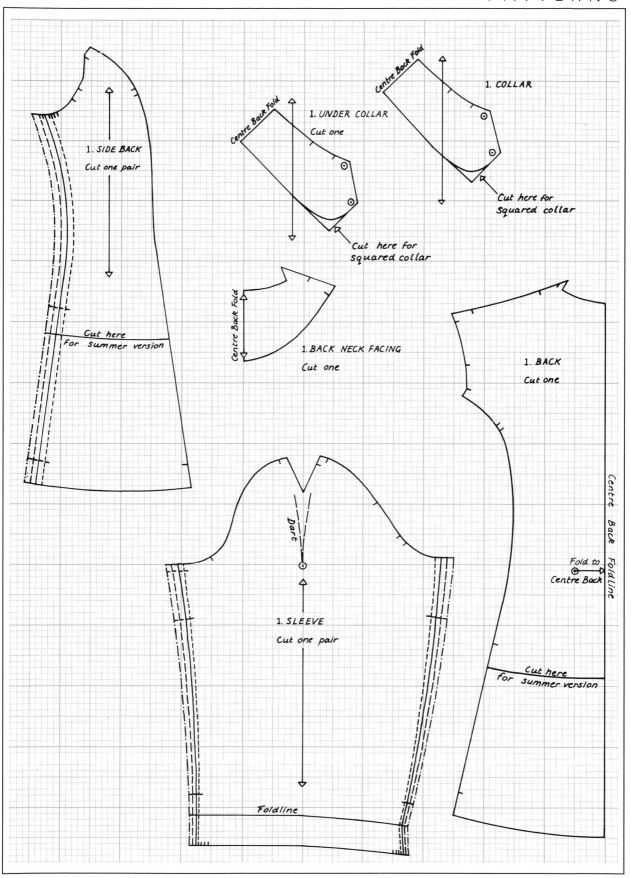

1. SIDE BACK

Cut one pair

Cut here
For summer version

1. UNDER COLLAR

Cut one

Centre Back Fold

Cut here for
squared collar

1. COLLAR

Centre Back Fold

Cut here for
Squared collar

1. BACK NECK FACING

Cut one

Centre Back Fold

1. BACK

Cut one

Centre Back Foldline

Fold to
Centre Back

Cut here
for summer version

Dart

1. SLEEVE

Cut one pair

Foldline

# STRAIGHT SKIRT

*Illustrated on page 22*

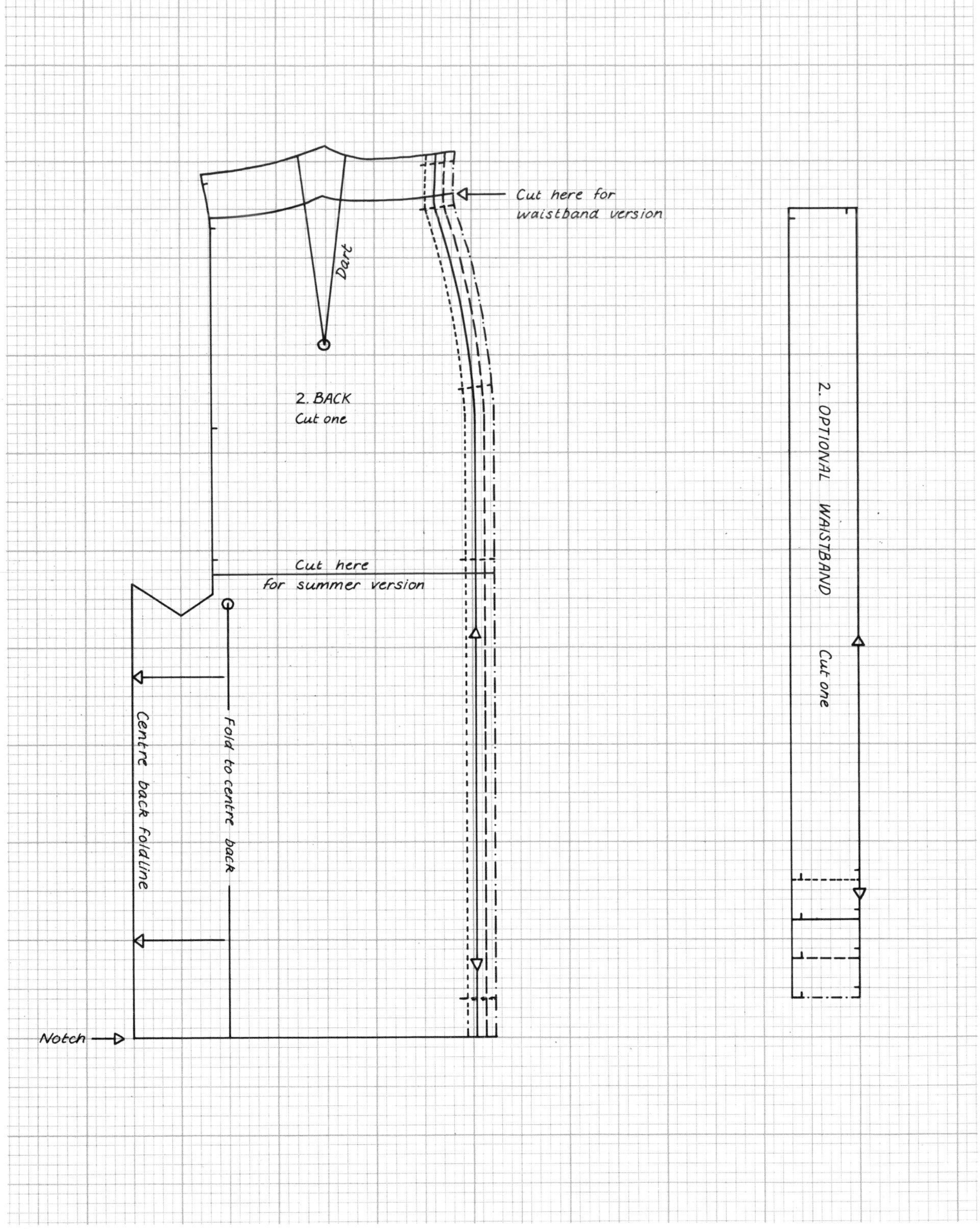

Cut here for
waistband version

Dart

2. BACK
Cut one

Cut here
for summer version

Centre back fold line

Fold to centre back

2. OPTIONAL WAISTBAND   Cut one

Notch

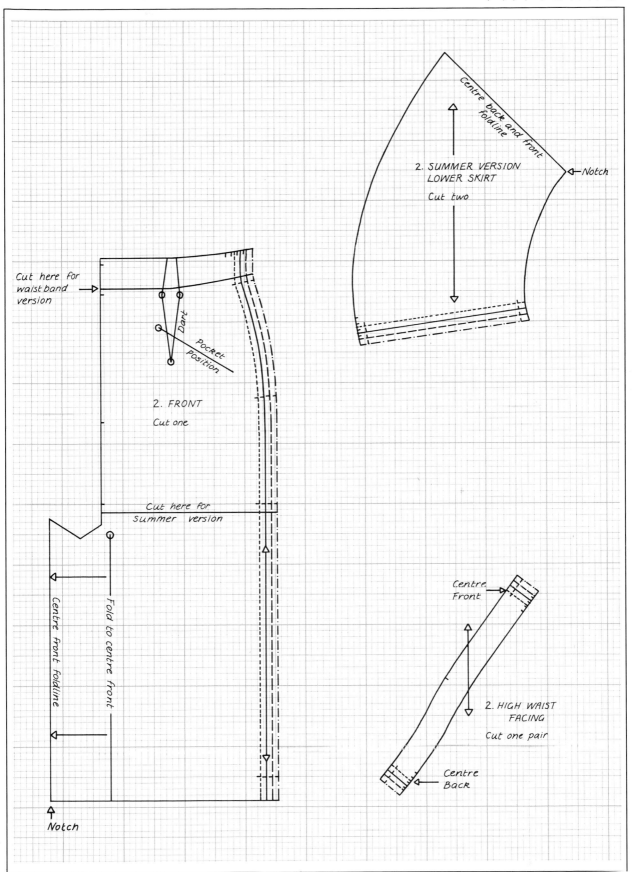

# WRAP BLOUSE

*Illustrated on page 26*

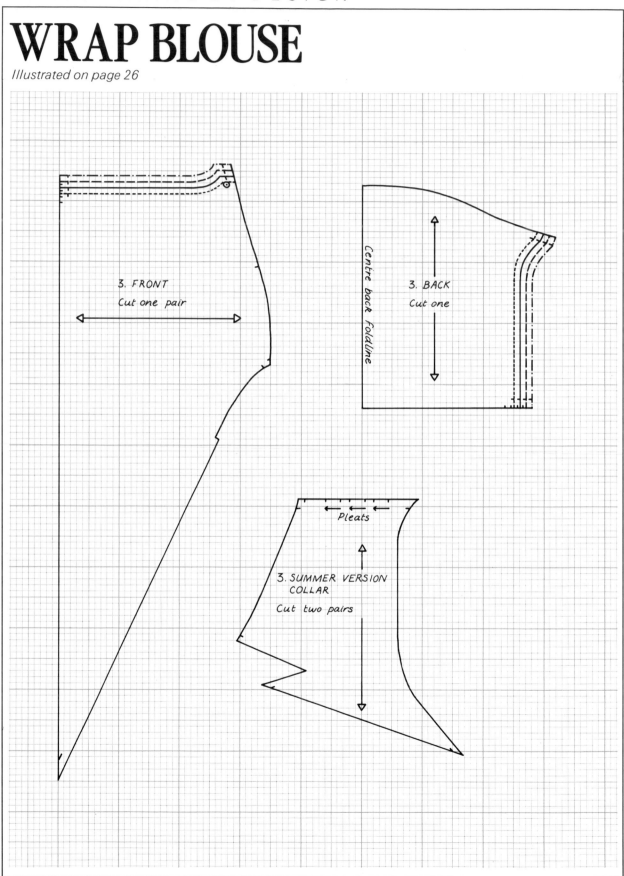

3. FRONT

Cut one pair

3. BACK

Cut one

Centre back foldline

Pleats

3. SUMMER VERSION
COLLAR

Cut two pairs

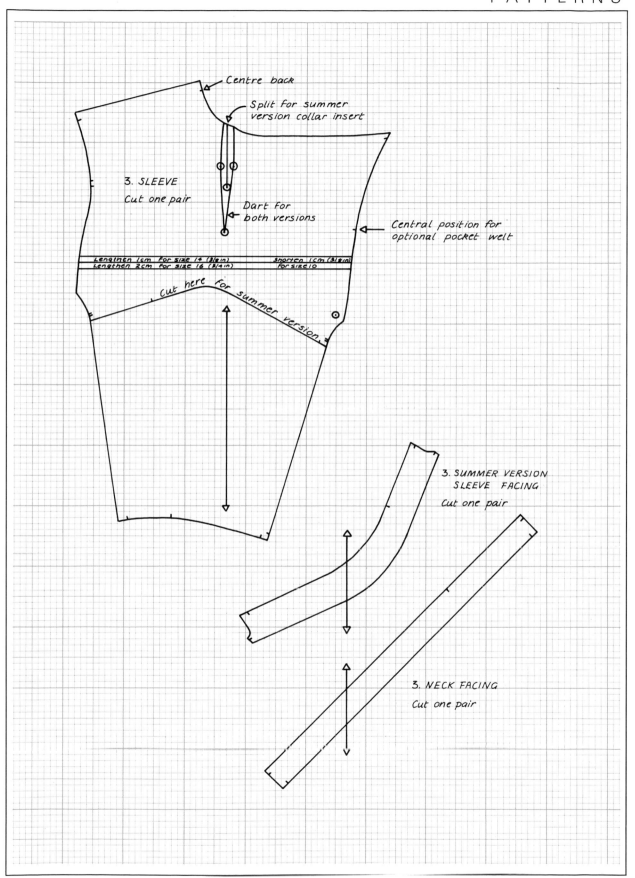

Centre back

Split for summer
version collar insert

3. SLEEVE
Cut one pair

Dart for
both versions

Central position for
optional pocket welt

| Lengthen 1cm for size 14 (3/8 in) | Shorten 1cm (3/8 in) |
| Lengthen 2cm for size 16 (3/4 in) | for size 10 |

Cut here for summer version

3. SUMMER VERSION
SLEEVE FACING
Cut one pair

3. NECK FACING
Cut one pair

# WRAP SKIRT

*Illustrated on page 30*

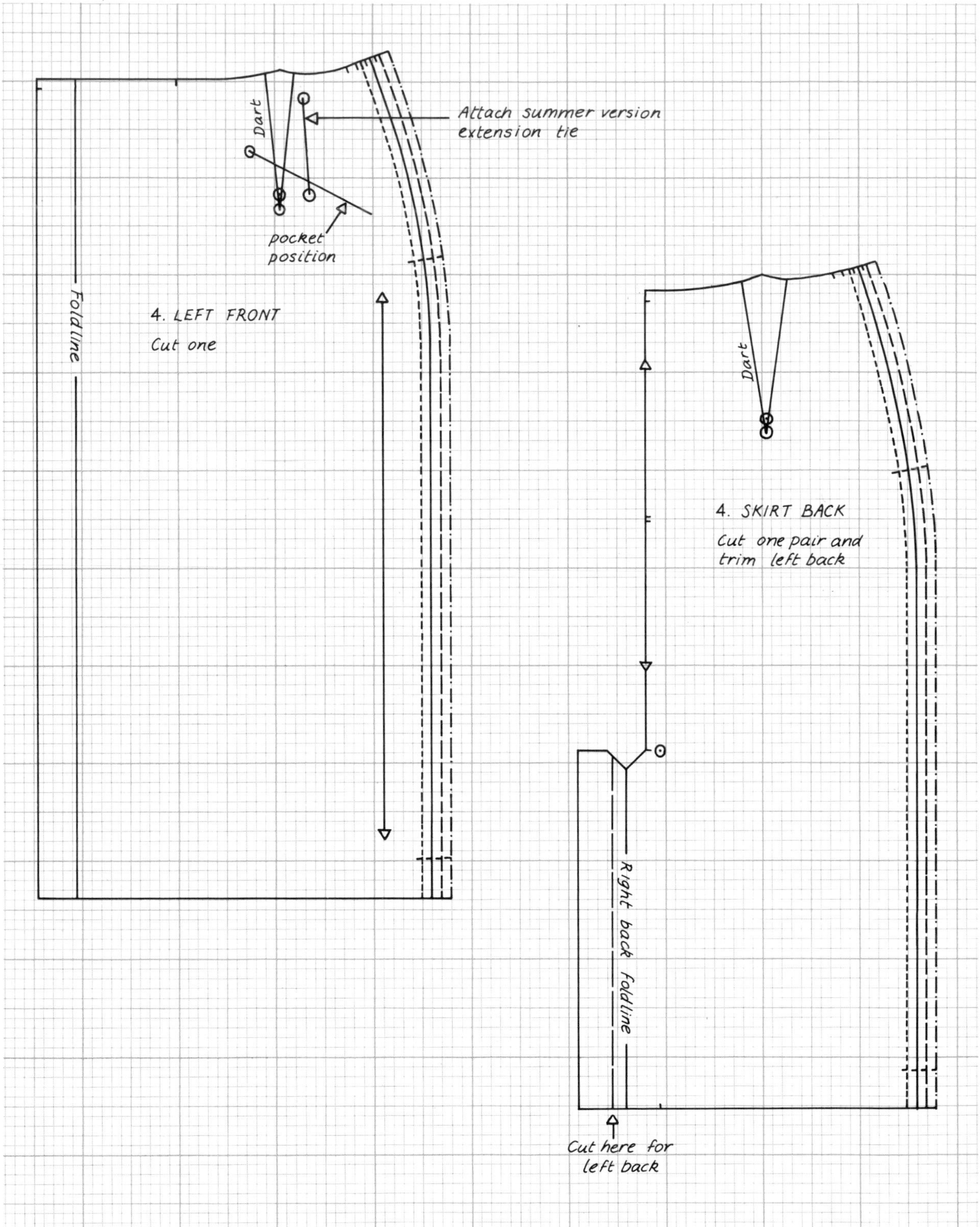

Dart

Attach summer version
extension tie

pocket
position

Foldline

4. LEFT FRONT

Cut one

Dart

4. SKIRT BACK

Cut one pair and
trim left back

Right back foldline

Cut here for
left back

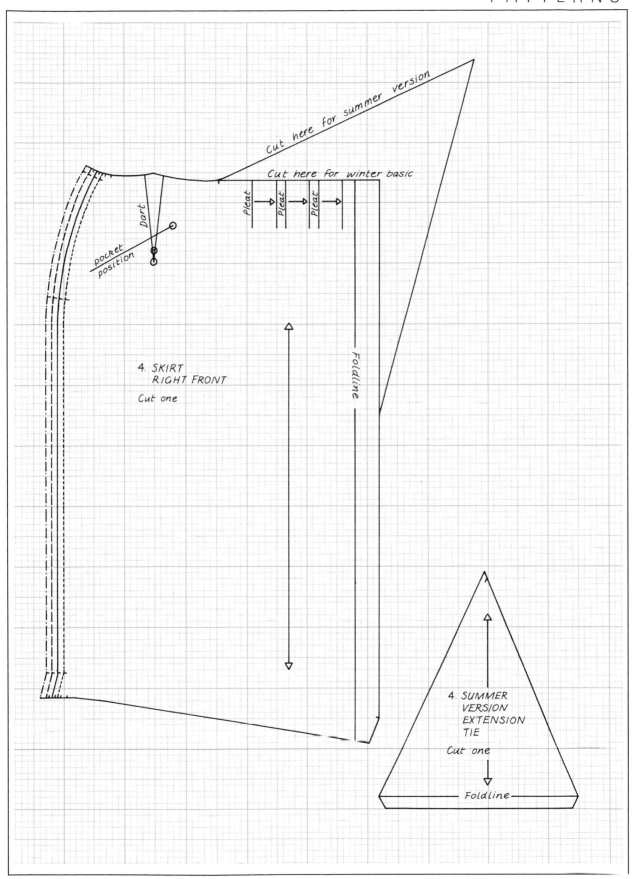

Cut here for summer version

Cut here for winter basic

Pleat →  Pleat →  Pleat →

Dart

pocket
position

Foldline

4. SKIRT
RIGHT FRONT

Cut one

4. SUMMER
VERSION
EXTENSION
TIE

Cut one

Foldline

# BLAZER

*Illustrated on page 38*

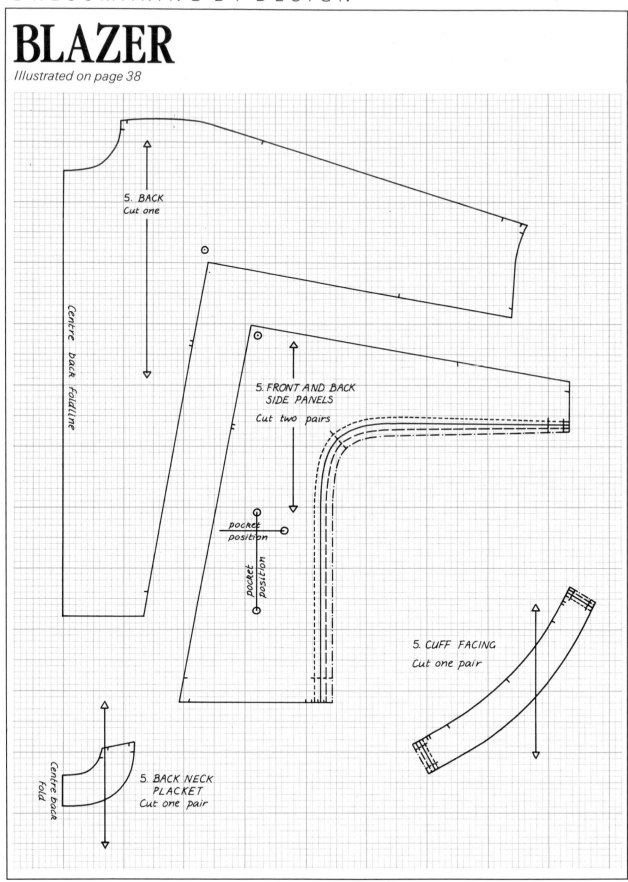

5. BACK
Cut one

Centre back foldline

5. FRONT AND BACK
SIDE PANELS

Cut two pairs

pocket
position

pocket
position

5. CUFF FACING

Cut one pair

Centre back
fold

5. BACK NECK
PLACKET
Cut one pair

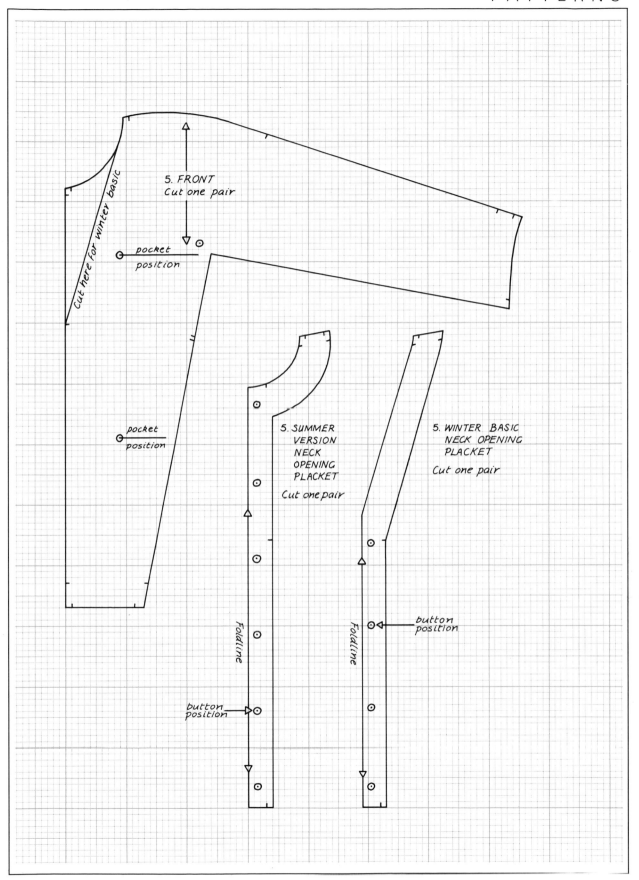

Cut here for winter basic

5. FRONT
Cut one pair

pocket
position

pocket
position

5. SUMMER
VERSION
NECK
OPENING
PLACKET

Cut one pair

5. WINTER BASIC
NECK OPENING
PLACKET

Cut one pair

Foldline

Foldline

button
position

button
position

# CASUAL TOP

*Illustrated on page 42*

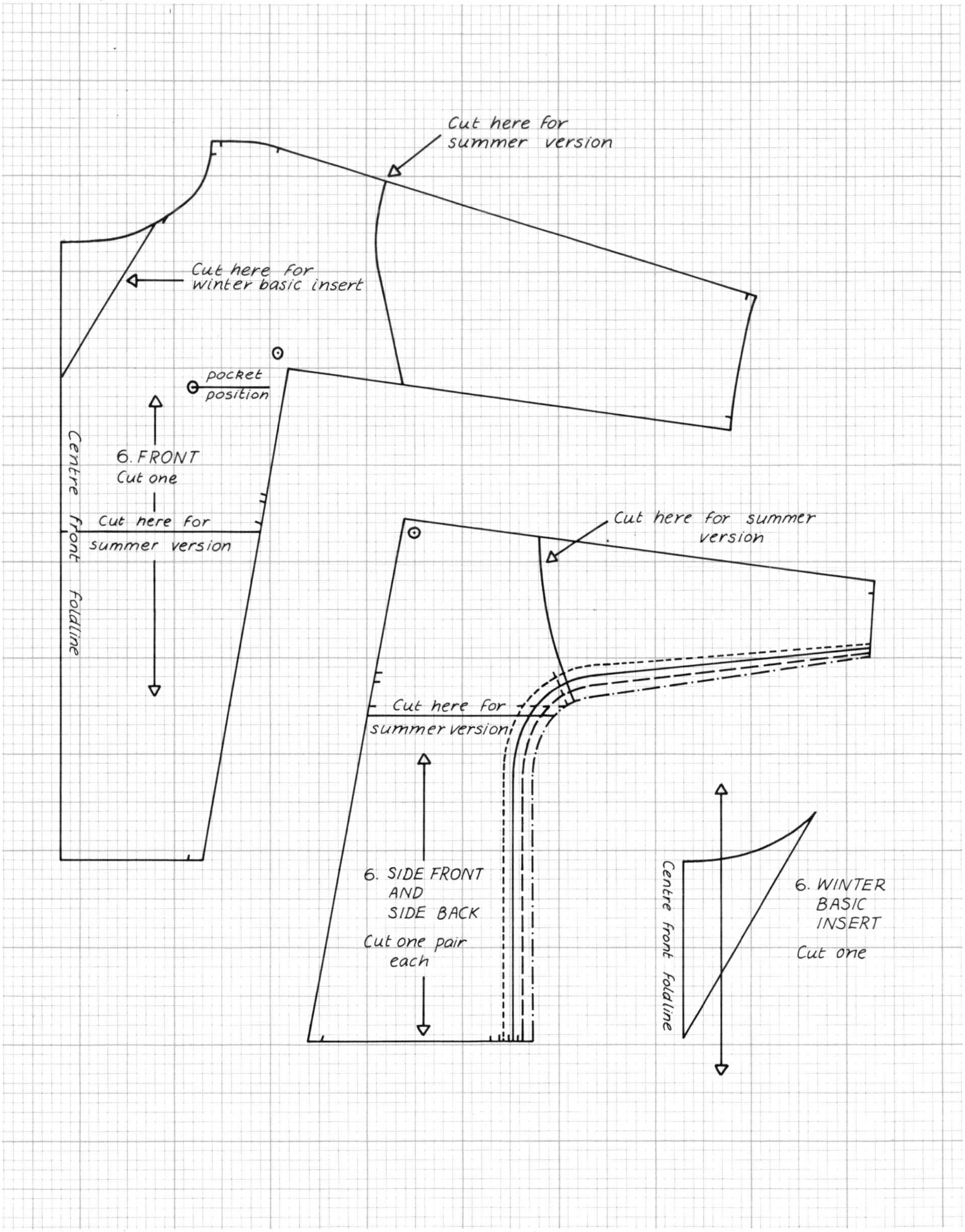

Cut here for
summer version

Cut here for
winter basic insert

pocket
position

Centre front Foldline

6. FRONT
Cut one

Cut here for
summer version

Cut here for summer
version

Cut here for
summer version

6. SIDE FRONT
AND
SIDE BACK

Cut one pair
each

Centre front Foldline

6. WINTER
BASIC
INSERT

Cut one

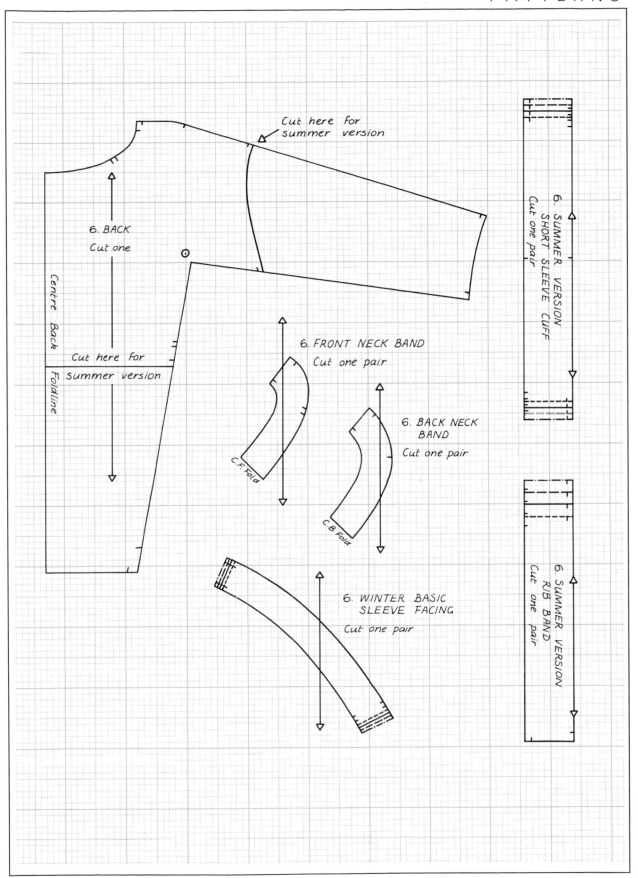

Cut here for
summer version

6. BACK

Cut one

Centre Back

Foldline

Cut here for
summer version

6. FRONT NECK BAND

Cut one pair

C.F. Fold

6. BACK NECK
BAND

Cut one pair

C.B. Fold

6. WINTER BASIC
SLEEVE FACING

Cut one pair

6. SUMMER VERSION
SHORT SLEEVE CUFF
Cut one pair

6. SUMMER VERSION
RIB BAND
Cut one pair

# PANTS

*Illustrated on page 46*

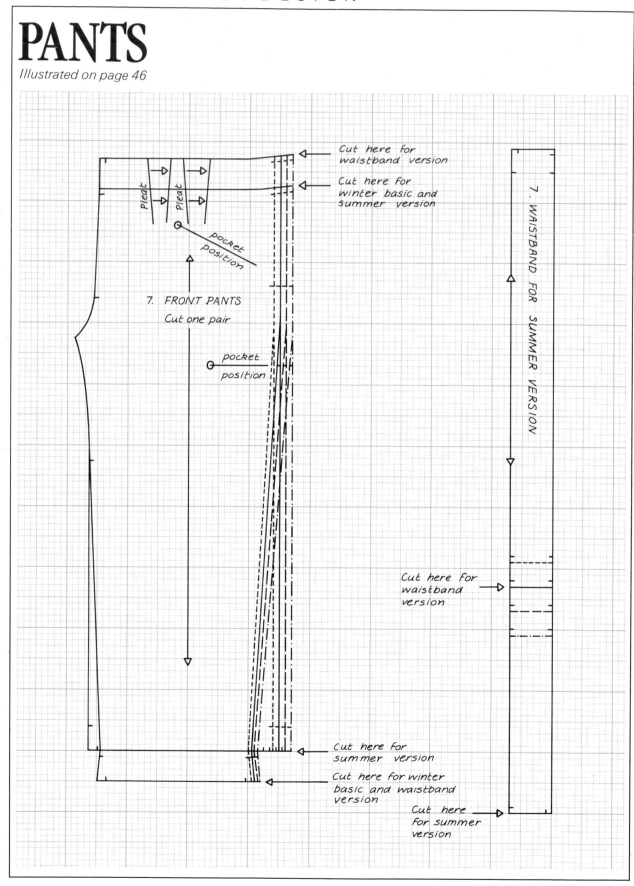

Cut here for waistband version

Cut here for winter basic and summer version

Pleat    Pleat

pocket position

7. FRONT PANTS

Cut one pair

pocket position

7. WAISTBAND FOR SUMMER VERSION

Cut here for waistband version

Cut here for summer version

Cut here for winter basic and waistband version

Cut here for summer version

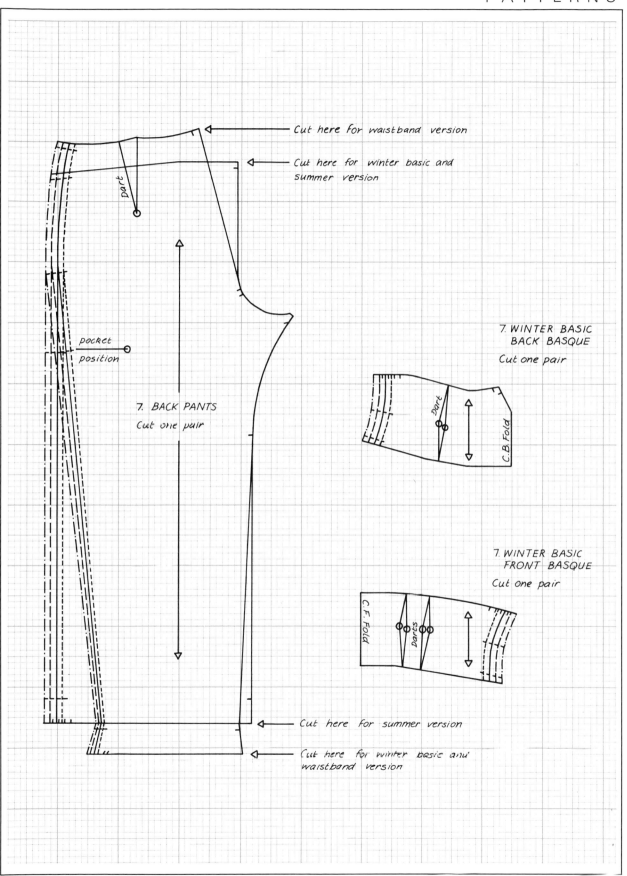

Cut here for waistband version

Cut here for winter basic and summer version

dart

pocket position

7. BACK PANTS
Cut one pair

7. WINTER BASIC BACK BASQUE
Cut one pair

Dart

C.B. Fold

7. WINTER BASIC FRONT BASQUE
Cut one pair

C.F. Fold

Darts

Cut here for summer version

Cut here for winter basic and waistband version

**Coat continued**

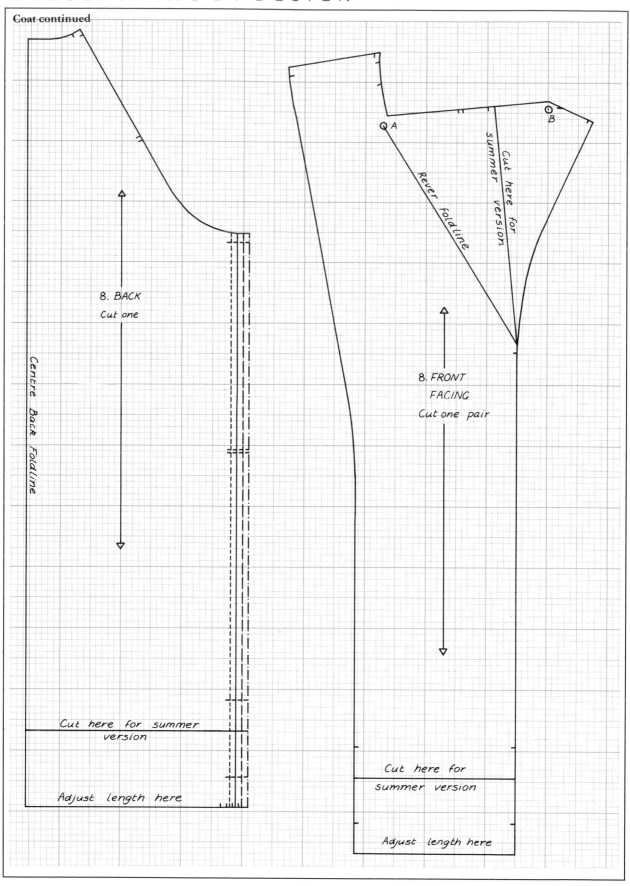

8. BACK
Cut one

Centre Back Foldline

Cut here for summer version

Adjust length here

Rever foldline

Cut here for summer version

○A

○B

8. FRONT FACING
Cut one pair

Cut here for summer version

Adjust length here

# SHAPED DRESS
*Illustrated on page 50*

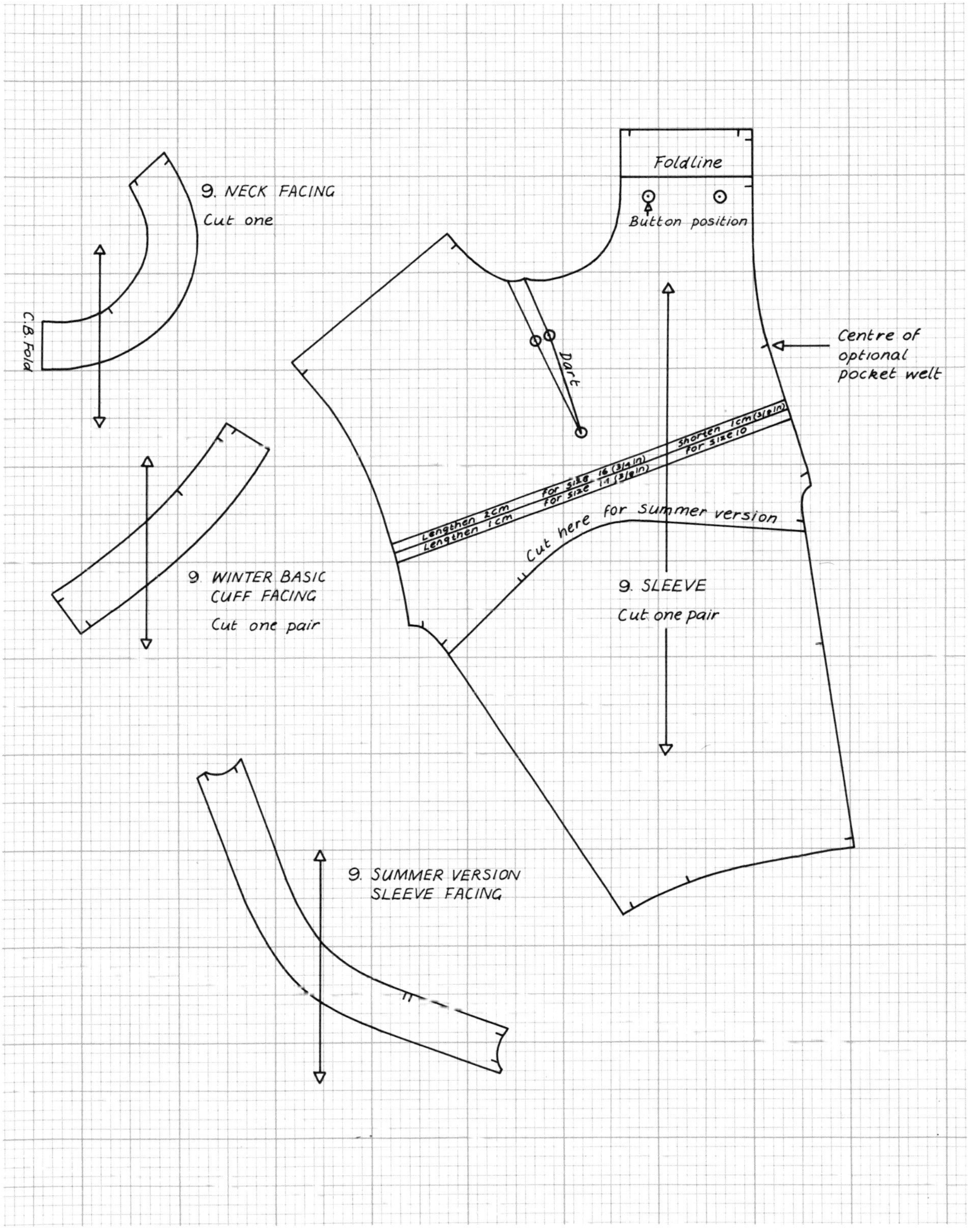

9. NECK FACING

Cut one

C.B. Fold

Foldline

Button position

Centre of
optional
pocket welt

Dart

Shorten 1cm (3/8 in)
for size 10

For size 16 (3/4 in)
For size 14 (3/8 in)

Lengthen 1cm
Lengthen 1cm

Cut here for Summer version

9. WINTER BASIC
CUFF FACING

Cut one pair

9. SLEEVE

Cut one pair

9. SUMMER VERSION
SLEEVE FACING

**Continued overleaf**

**Shaped dress continued**

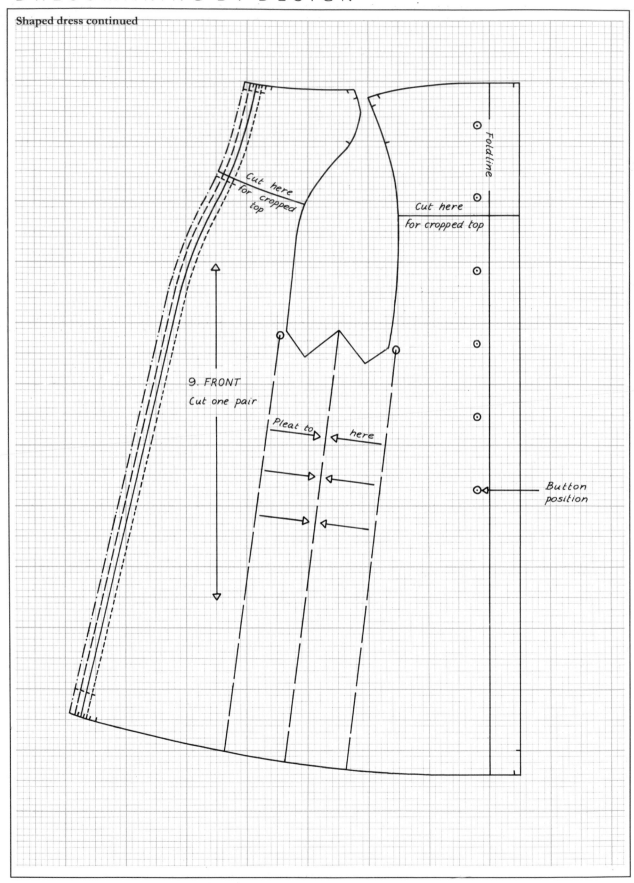

Cut here for cropped top

Cut here for cropped top

Foldline

9. FRONT

Cut one pair

Pleat to here

Button position

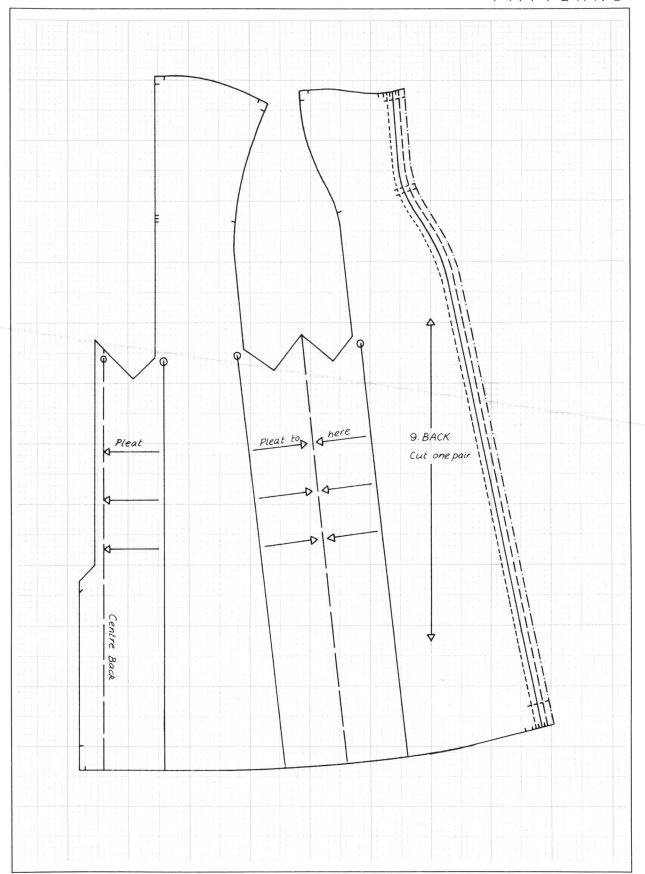

Pleat

Pleat to → ← here

9. BACK
Cut one pair

Centre Back

# FULL SKIRT

*Illustrated on page 54*

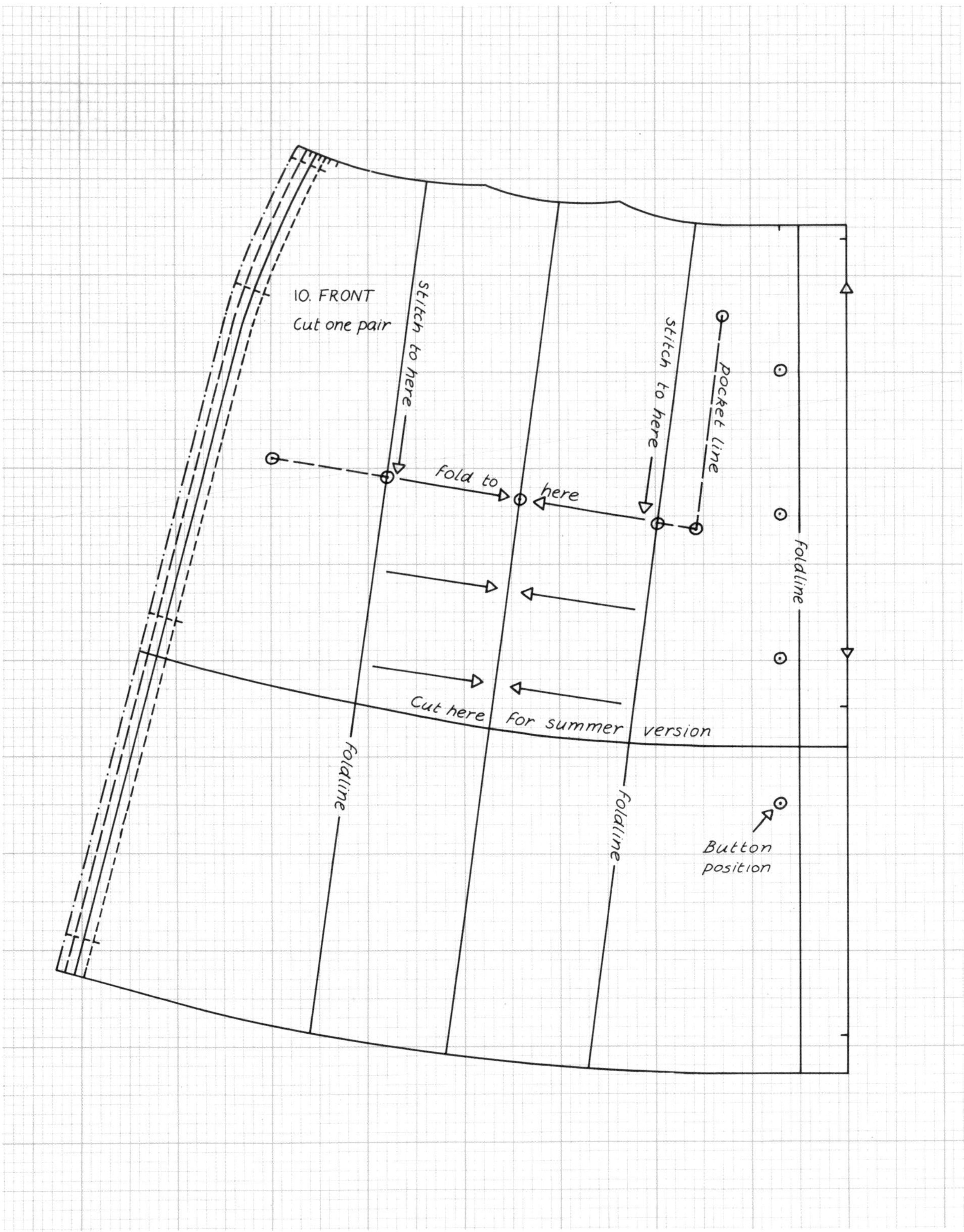

10. FRONT
Cut one pair

Stitch to here

stitch to here

pocket line

fold to here

Foldline

Foldline

Foldline

Cut here for summer version

Button position

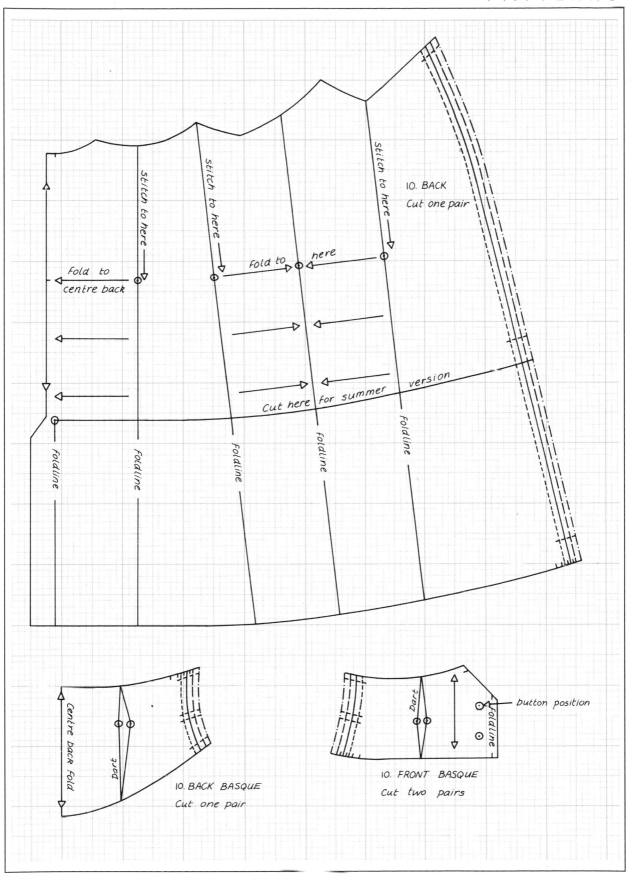

fold to
centre back

Stitch to here

stitch to here

stitch to here

Stitch to here

10. BACK
Cut one pair

fold to here

Cut here for summer version

Foldline

Foldline

Foldline

Foldline

Foldline

Centre back fold

Dart

10. BACK BASQUE
Cut one pair

Dart

Foldline

button position

10. FRONT BASQUE
Cut two pairs

# SHIRT
*Illustrated on page 58*

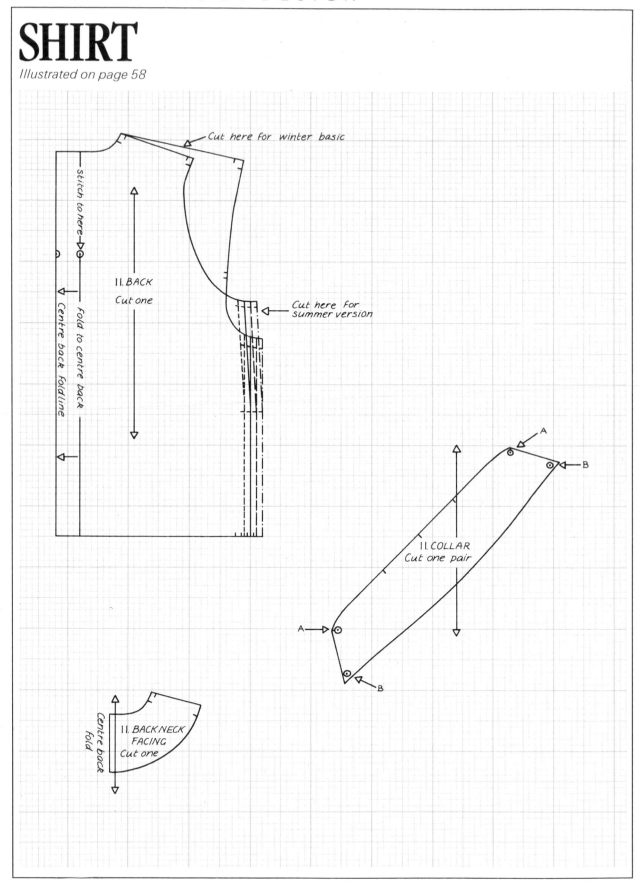

Cut here for winter basic

Stitch to here →

Fold to centre back

Centre back foldline

11. BACK
Cut one

Cut here for summer version

A

B

11. COLLAR
Cut one pair

A →

B

Centre back fold

11. BACK NECK FACING
Cut one

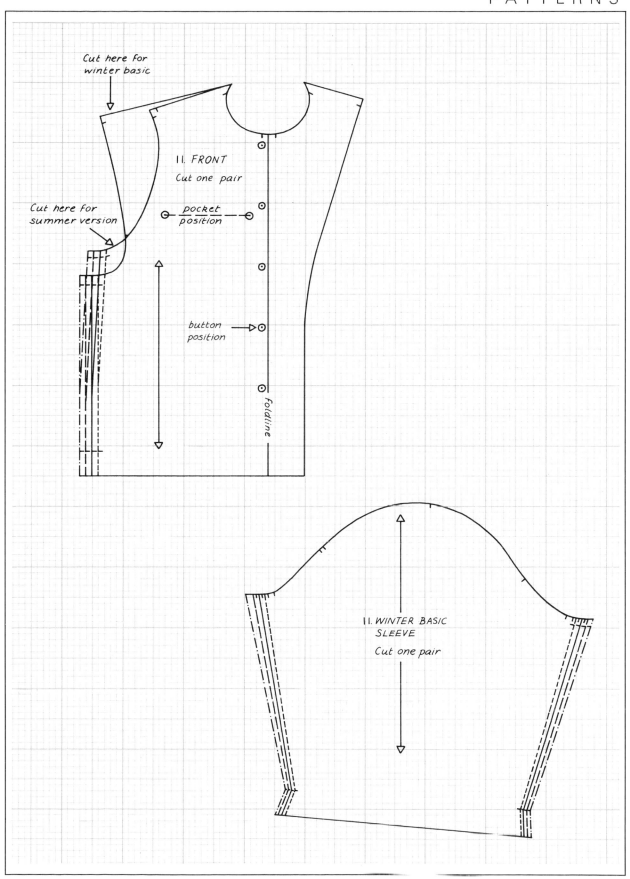

Cut here for
winter basic

11. FRONT
Cut one pair

Cut here for
summer version

pocket
position

button
position

Foldline

11. WINTER BASIC
SLEEVE

Cut one pair

# MACINTOSH

*Illustrated on page 62*

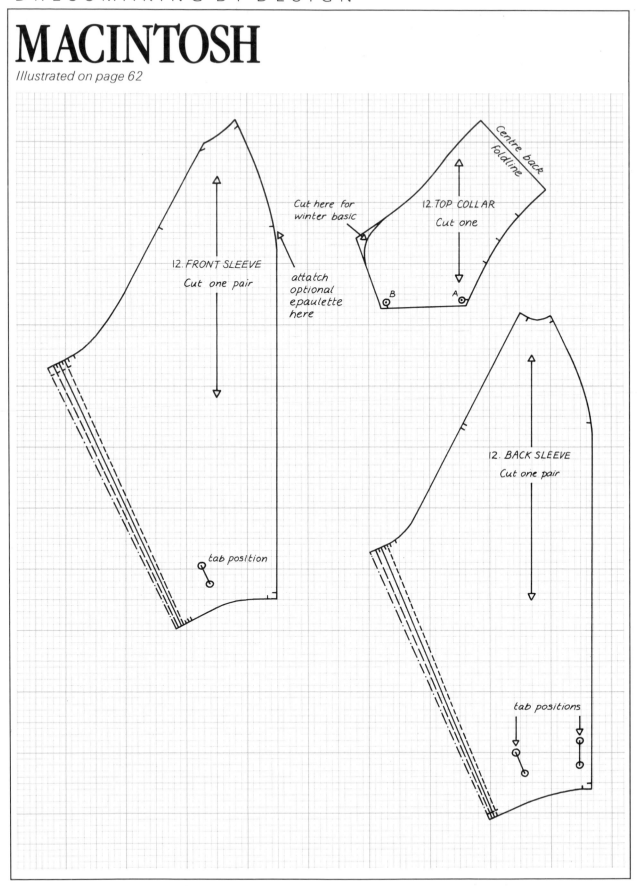

12. FRONT SLEEVE

Cut one pair

Cut here for
winter basic

attatch
optional
epaulette
here

12. TOP COLLAR

Cut one

Centre back
foldline

B

A

tab position

12. BACK SLEEVE

Cut one pair

tab positions

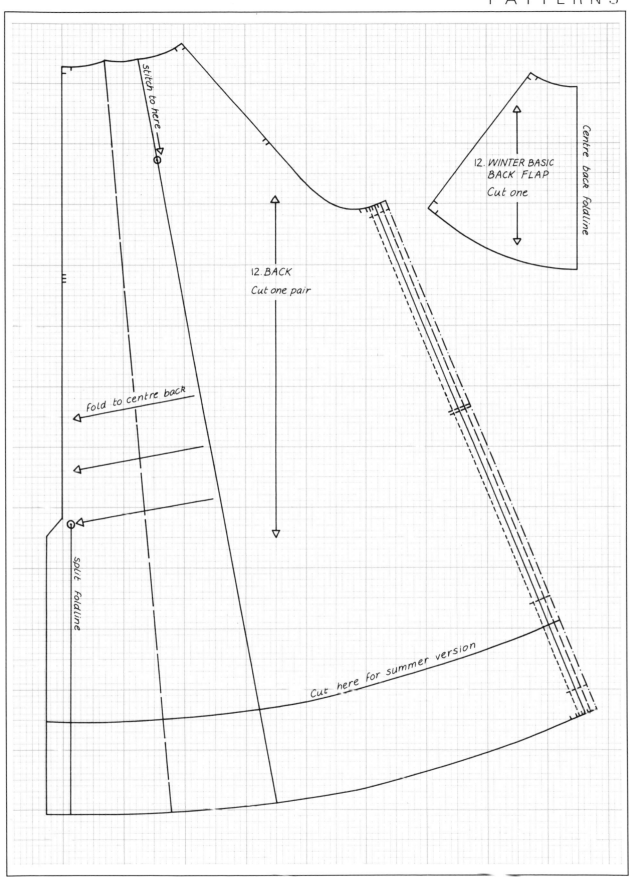

stitch to here

12. WINTER BASIC
BACK FLAP

Cut one

Centre back foldline

12. BACK

Cut one pair

fold to centre back

Split Foldline

Cut here for summer version

**Macintosh continued**

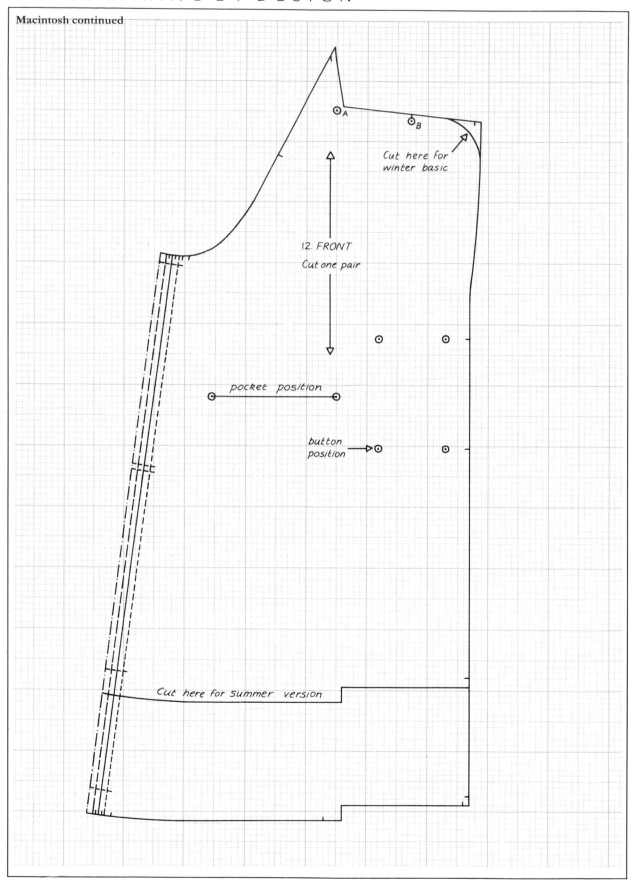

12. FRONT

Cut one pair

Cut here for winter basic

pocket position

button position

Cut here for summer version

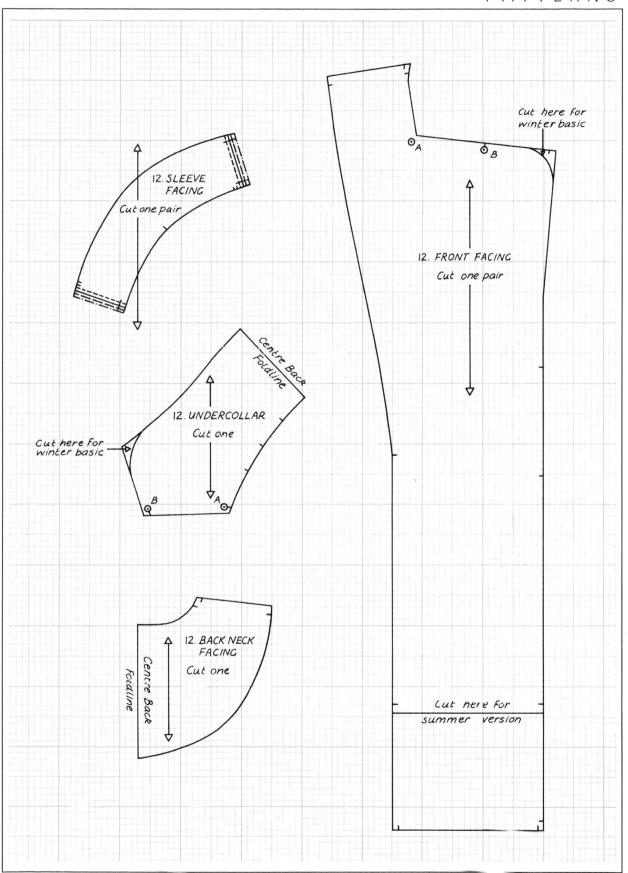

12. SLEEVE FACING

Cut one pair

12. FRONT FACING

Cut one pair

Cut here for winter basic

Centre Back Foldline

12. UNDERCOLLAR

Cut one

Cut here for winter basic

B

A

12. BACK NECK FACING

Cut one

Centre Back Foldline

Cut here for summer version

# FINISHING DETAILS

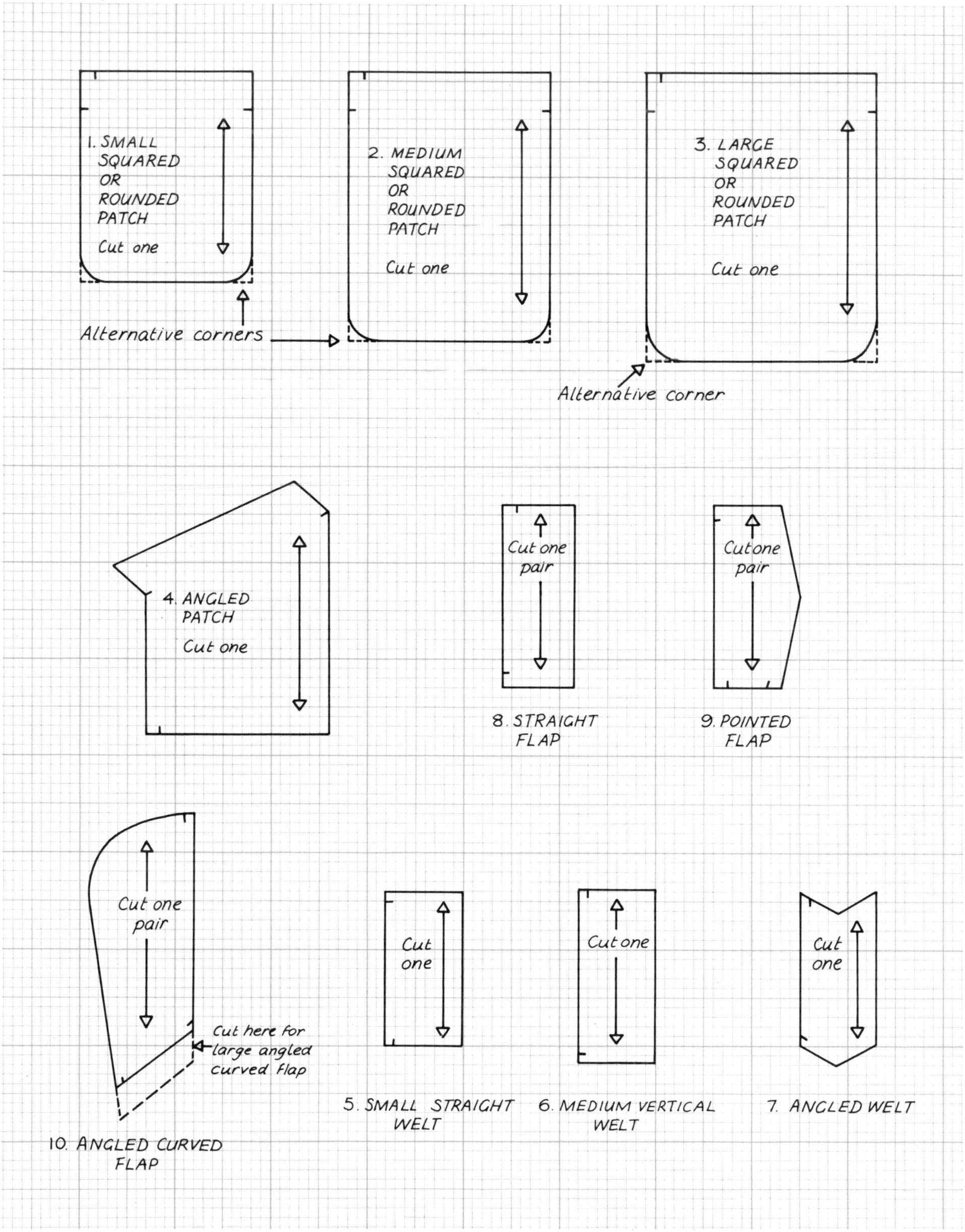

1. SMALL SQUARED OR ROUNDED PATCH

Cut one

2. MEDIUM SQUARED OR ROUNDED PATCH

Cut one

3. LARGE SQUARED OR ROUNDED PATCH

Cut one

Alternative corners →

Alternative corner

4. ANGLED PATCH

Cut one

Cut one pair

8. STRAIGHT FLAP

Cut one pair

9. POINTED FLAP

Cut one pair

Cut here for large angled curved flap

10. ANGLED CURVED FLAP

Cut one

5. SMALL STRAIGHT WELT

Cut one

6. MEDIUM VERTICAL WELT

Cut one

7. ANGLED WELT

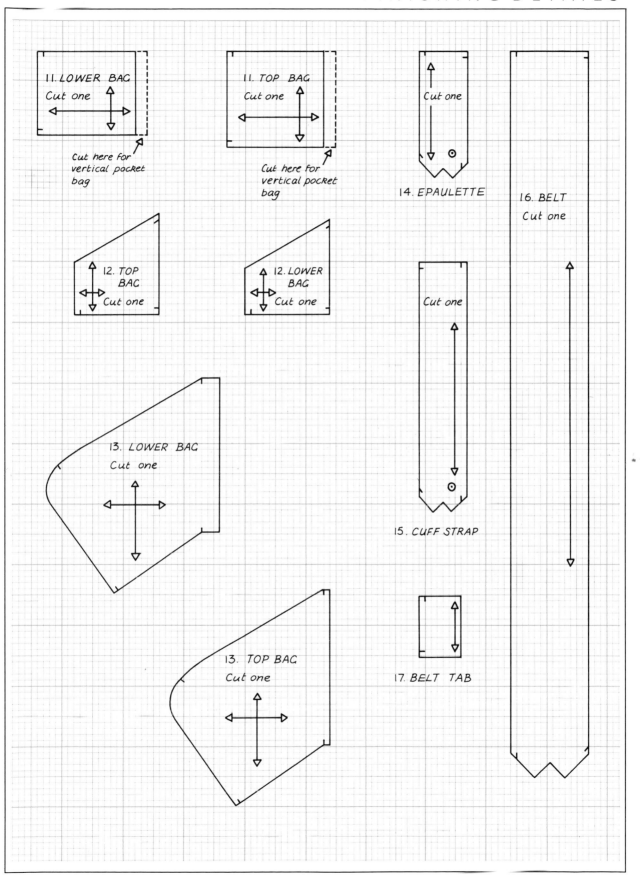

11. LOWER BAG
Cut one

Cut here for vertical pocket bag

11. TOP BAG
Cut one

Cut here for vertical pocket bag

Cut one

14. EPAULETTE

16. BELT
Cut one

12. TOP BAG
Cut one

12. LOWER BAG
Cut one

Cut one

15. CUFF STRAP

13. LOWER BAG
Cut one

13. TOP BAG
Cut one

17. BELT TAB

# FINISHING DETAILS

This section has been specifically planned so that you can use any one of these details, or a combination, to finish off your design as you choose. You can change the whole style of a garment with clever use of details. Welt pockets give a more tailored finish, for example, while patch pockets look more casual. You can also add pocket flaps to pockets to create a different finish.

If you want to add or adjust a detail, simply cut out a paper pattern of the detail you intend to use and pin it against the pattern of the garment you are making. Adjust the height and position to suit your shape, then mark the position of each paper pattern piece before removing it to cut out and make-up. As far as possible, check the full effect in the mirror before sewing the finishing details in place.

## SMALL PATCH POCKETS, SQUARE OR ROUNDED

**Finished measurement:** 15 cm (6 in) wide by 16.5 cm ($6\frac{1}{2}$ in) deep.
**You will need:** 30 cm (12 in) fabric.

### Cut out fabric

**1** Draw up pattern from page 106, following the instructions on page 114. Cut out required number of pockets.

### Neaten edges

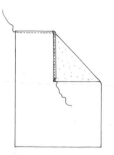

**2** Neaten top raw edge of pocket by folding 5 mm ($\frac{1}{4}$ in) to wrong side and stitching across.

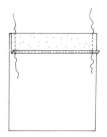

**3** Fold neatened top edge of pocket over, following notch marks, right sides together, to form facing. Stitch down each short side, taking 1.5 cm ($\frac{5}{8}$ in) seams.

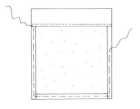

**4** Turn facing to right side and neaten around remaining three raw edges of pocket, turning under seam allowance in line with stitching at end of facing. Baste and press. For rounded pockets, allow curved seam allowances at lower corners to form small, even folds.

**5** On wrong side, edgestitch along neatened inner edge of facing, through to right side, stitching from one side to the other. Press.

## Attach to garment

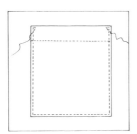

**6** Attach pocket to main fabric as marked and baste into position. Edgestitch around sides and bottom of pocket, beginning and ending with a small wedge shape at each side of the top opening to strengthen. Press.

## MEDIUM PATCH POCKETS, SQUARE OR ROUNDED

**Finished measurement:** 18 cm (7 in) wide by 22.5 cm (9 in) deep.
**You will need:** 35 cm (14 in) fabric.

Cut out and make up as for small patch pocket (no. 1).

## LARGE PATCH POCKETS

**Finished measurement:** 21 cm ($8\frac{1}{4}$ in) wide by 24.5 cm ($9\frac{5}{8}$ in) deep.
**You will need:** 35 cm (14 in) fabric.

Cut out and make up as for small patch pocket (no. 1).

## ANGLED PATCH POCKETS

**Finished measurement:** 19 cm ($7\frac{1}{2}$ in) wide across opening, 16 cm ($6\frac{3}{8}$ in) wide across lower edge, 21 cm ($8\frac{1}{8}$ in) deep at deepest point.
**You will need:** 30 cm (12 in) fabric.

### Cut out fabric

**1** Draw up pattern pieces from page 106, following the instructions on page 114. Cut out a pair of pockets from a folded, double thickness of fabric.

**2** Neaten edges and attach to garment as for small patch pockets (no. 1).

## STRAIGHT POCKET FLAP

**Finished measurement:** 16 cm ($6\frac{3}{8}$ in) wide by 4.5 cm ($1\frac{3}{4}$ in) deep, to go with small patch pocket (no. 1) or squared pocket bag (no. 11).
**You will need:** 25 cm (10 in) fabric, plus interfacing (optional).

### Cut out fabric

**1** Draw up pattern piece from page 106. For each flap, cut out one pair of pieces in fabric.

### Make up flap

**2** Apply optional interfacing to wrong side of top flap only.

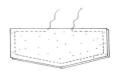

**3** Attach top to underflap, right sides together and raw edges and notches matching. Stitch all round, beginning along the top of the flap and working around corners to finish at the top, leaving a 5 cm (2 in) gap through which to turn (shown here with a pointed flap).

**4** Trim corners, clip curves and turn to right side. Press. Close top turning gap with slipstitches (see Sewing techniques, page 119) and press again.

**5** Edgestitch or topstitch to match main garment, around sides and bottom flap only. Make optional buttonholes.

## Attach to garment

**6** Attach flap to main fabric as marked, positioning top edge 1 cm ($\frac{3}{8}$ in) above pocket line or any patch pocket already in place. Baste.

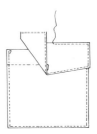

**7** Set in pocket bag, if required (see over). Edgestitch or slipstitch across top edge of flap and then press.

## EPAULETTES

**Finished measurement:** 19 cm (7½ in) long by 3 cm (1¼ in) wide.
**You will need:** 25 cm (10 in) fabric plus interfacing (optional).

### Cut out fabric

**1** Draw up pattern pieces from page 107 and cut out one piece in fabric for each epaulette.

### Make up epaulette

**2** Apply optional interfacing to wrong side of epaulette.

**3** Fold epaulette lengthways, right sides together so that raw edges match. Stitch around point and down one long side. Trim seam allowance at point, turn right side out and press.

**4** Turn in short raw ends of epaulette and slipstitch (see Sewing techniques, page 119) across to close. On right side, edgestitch around two long sides and point of epaulette.

**5** Make buttonhole at marked position at point of epaulette.

## Attach to garment

**6** Pin epaulette to garment, top of epaulette facing right side of garment, centrally over shoulder seam, with point of epaulette towards sleeve.

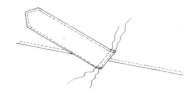

**7** Edgestitch across base and through shoulder line to set, then stitch again across base, 1.5 cm (⅝ in) from edge, parallel to first line of stitching.

**8** Fold epaulette back into position, pointing towards neckline. Attach button on shoulder line to match buttonhole. For an extra detail add belt tabs (no. 17), attaching them across the shoulder line of each sleeve, over the rows of stitching so that epaulette can be threaded over it.

## CUFF STRAP

**Finished measurement:** 39 cm (15⅜ in) long by 3 cm (1¼ in) wide.
**You will need:** 15 cm (6 in) fabric, plus interfacing (optional).

### Cut out and make up

**1** Cut out and make up cuff strap exactly as for epaulettes (no. 14).

### Attach to cuff

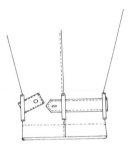

**2** Attach button to blunt end of each strap to fit snugly round wrist, then thread through belt tabs (no. 17) to finish.

## BELT

**Finished measurement:** 118 cm (46¼ in) long by 5.5 cm (2⅛ in) wide. **You will need:** 20 cm (47 in) fabric plus interfacing or belt stiffening (optional).

### Cut out and make up

**1** Make up belt exactly as for epaulettes (no. 14).

### Finish belt

**2** Attach buckle to blunt end of belt, wrapping it to wrong side through the centre of the buckle and stitching by hand or with a double row of machine stitches set 1 cm (⅜ in) apart, across the back of the belt end to set in place. Attach optional belt tabs.

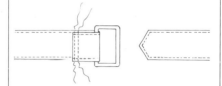

## BELT TABS

**Finished measurement:** 8 cm (3⅛ in) long by 5 cm (2 in) wide. Adjust length if necessary. **You will need:** 10 cm (4 in) fabric.

### Cut out fabric

**1** Draw up pattern piece from page 107 and cut out required number of tabs in fabric.

### Make up tabs

**2** Fold 1 cm (⅜ in) to wrong side down each long side of tab and press.

**3** Fold under 1 cm (⅜ in) to wrong side at each short end of tab and press.

**4** Fold tab in half lengthways to enclose all seam allowances and press.

**5** Edgestitch down both long edges of tab.

### Attach to garment

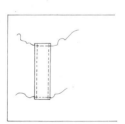

**6** Attach tab to main fabric and edgestitch across top and bottom short ends to close and secure firmly to fabric.

# INDEX